LILLIAN TOO'S
FENG SHUI
SYMBOLS OF GOOD FORTUNE

ALL THE SYMBOLS OF GOOD FORTUNE TO:

JAZZ UP YOUR LOVE LIFE

LET YOU LIVE TO A RIPE OLD AGE

INCREASE YOUR CAREER LUCK

BRING YOU FAME & RECOGNITION

GIVE YOU WONDERFUL CHILDREN

LET YOU STAY HEALTHY

INCREASE YOUR POPULARITY

NURTURE YOU A HAPPY FAMILY and...

HELP YOU BECOME SERIOUSLY RICH

KONSEP BOOKS
KONSEP LAGENDA SDN BHD (223 855)
Kuala Lumpur 59100 Malaysia.

WEBSITES:
www.lillian-too.com
www.wofs.com
Email: ltoo@wofs.com

Lillian Too's Symbols of Good Fortune

ISBN 983 9778-08-0
First published in June 1999
and reprinted fourteen times.
Improved edition April 2003
Reprint February 2004
Reprint May 2004
This revised edition April 2007

Symbolism is very much an integral and all-encompassing part of feng shui practice and interpretation. Yet is usually overlooked and frequently brushed aside as superstition and old wives' tales.

Symbolism is about knowing and understanding the meanings of objects, structures and elements. It incorporates popular attributes and characteristics of flowers, animals, creatures, birds and objects et al into enhancing one's personal space and environment, thereby attracting good fortune. Protective symbols also wards off misfortunes caused by bad feng shui or by bad astrological periods. Symbolism thus gives substance to feng shui practice.

This book is meant to be a useful supplement to all the formulas and techniques of feng shui practice already covered in my other books. Symbolism brings depth to feng shui practice. It is also very practical and very easy. Yet it is as potent as the formulas that require more complex study!

As an enthusiastic collector of Chinese paintings, ceramics, urns, sculptures, figurines and so forth I developed keen interest in the meanings of all good fortune symbols featured in these works of arts, crafts and furniture. I discovered that incorporating my knowledge of symbolism into my feng shui practice greatly enhanced the effectiveness of my practice. I also found the presence of, for instance the Laughing Buddha or the Pi Yao; very assuring for overcoming annual afflictions.

In 2006, I placed a 5-element pagoda in the West to overcome the 5 Yellow there and this helped me (a Rooster) go through the year safely. In the same way by placing a Pi Yao and lots of green plants in the Southeast, I appeased the Grand Duke Jupiter there and various projects of mine went smoothly despite being hurt by the Grand Duke.

Symbolism plays a huge part in the practical applications of feng shui and displaying good fortune symbols in any home or office correctly, speeds up the onset of good fortune brought about by good feng shui orientations.

The Laughing Buddha, also known as the Buddha of Happiness, is famous for transforming people's problems into happiness.

Lots of Green Plants always symbolize wood energy and can be used to enhance the SE and East, or counter particularly fierce malevolent earth stars.

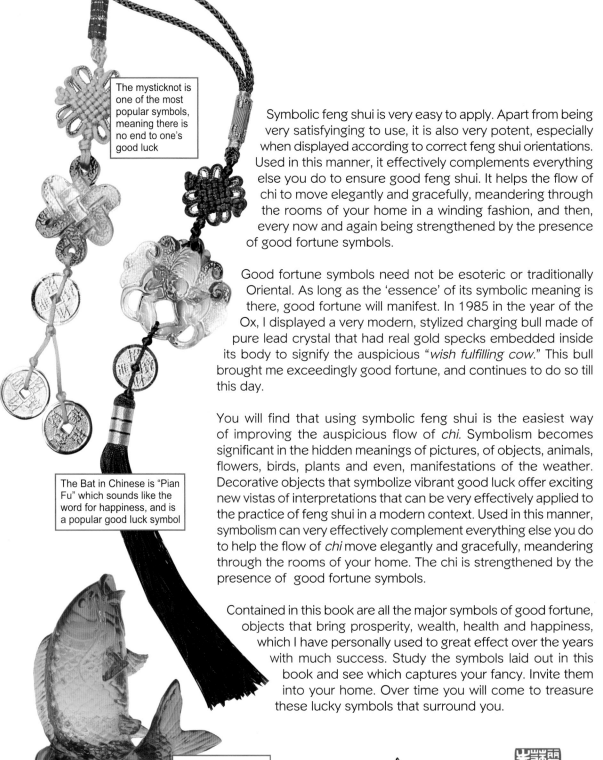

The mysticknot is one of the most popular symbols, meaning there is no end to one's good luck

The Bat in Chinese is "Pian Fu" which sounds like the word for happiness, and is a popular good luck symbol

Fish always mean abundance. A fish depicted jumping in this manner symbolises crossing the Dragon Gate which indicates great success.

Symbolic feng shui is very easy to apply. Apart from being very satisfyinging to use, it is also very potent, especially when displayed according to correct feng shui orientations. Used in this manner, it effectively complements everything else you do to ensure good feng shui. It helps the flow of chi to move elegantly and gracefully, meandering through the rooms of your home in a winding fashion, and then, every now and again being strengthened by the presence of good fortune symbols.

Good fortune symbols need not be esoteric or traditionally Oriental. As long as the 'essence' of its symbolic meaning is there, good fortune will manifest. In 1985 in the year of the Ox, I displayed a very modern, stylized charging bull made of pure lead crystal that had real gold specks embedded inside its body to signify the auspicious "wish fulfilling cow." This bull brought me exceedingly good fortune, and continues to do so till this day.

You will find that using symbolic feng shui is the easiest way of improving the auspicious flow of chi. Symbolism becomes significant in the hidden meanings of pictures, of objects, animals, flowers, birds, plants and even, manifestations of the weather. Decorative objects that symbolize vibrant good luck offer exciting new vistas of interpretations that can be very effectively applied to the practice of feng shui in a modern context. Used in this manner, symbolism can very effectively complement everything else you do to help the flow of chi move elegantly and gracefully, meandering through the rooms of your home. The chi is strengthened by the presence of good fortune symbols.

Contained in this book are all the major symbols of good fortune, objects that bring prosperity, wealth, health and happiness, which I have personally used to great effect over the years with much success. Study the symbols laid out in this book and see which captures your fancy. Invite them into your home. Over time you will come to treasure these lucky symbols that surround you.

Symbols Of Good Fortune

Contents

Opening notes

Introduction :
The Power of Symbols in Feng Shui

All Chinese characters and words are essentially pictures that communicate their meaning through the visual. Chinese words are more graphic than phonetic, reflecting the Chinese penchant for viewing most objects as containing hidden meanings that are symbolic of either good luck or misfortune. Thus they view many objects as conveyers of symbolic good or bad luck, and they view events as signs - portents of good or bad tidings.

Pictures and words are said to contain more meaning than is at first evident. And these meanings can be immediately obvious or they may be hidden. Usually, however, symbolic meanings are seldom grasped at first glance except by those who have learnt to look beyond the obvious.

Hidden meanings associated with objects and events often have greater potency than ordinary language can describe. The symbolism of Chinese beliefs is usually rich with nuances and contains multiple shades of meanings. Thus for example in a Chinese painting of landscape, there are meanings in the

way clouds, trees, mountains, rocks, streams, grass and the characters have been drawn in. To the untrained eye, the painting shows a scenic view, nothing more. But to the trained eye, expert in the hidden meanings of feng shui symbols, the way the clouds are shaped, the selection of trees, the positioning of the water, rocks and grass and finally the shape and orientation of mountains in the painting can indicate messages of goodwill.

There may either be plenty of prosperity meanings or there may be hidden poison arrows inadvertently placed there so the painting itself becomes an inauspicious purveyor of killing breath. Chinese artists of the old days were thus knowledgeable about the more popular good fortune symbols. This not only enhanced the marketability of their works but also increased their commissioned business.

> All oriental paintings are meant to be appreciated not simply as works of art. They must be viewed as conveying symbolic meanings. They have characteristic themes like longevity, prosperity, happiness and so forth, and these meanings are suggested not by words but by images.

Chinese paintings are almost always painted with auspicious themes so that they usually mean more than simply the images drawn. These images can be plants, trees, animals, flowers, mountains, deities or humans. There is virtually nothing in the whole of nature, organic or inorganic, no creature, no posture, no colour - which the Chinese painter does not view as being imbued with symbolic meaning. The skill of the artist lies not just in the way images are painted but also in the way images are combined. Those artists possessing of calligraphic talents would also ensure that both image and script would resonate with propitious meanings. Excellent calligraphy in itself - the beautiful rendition of good fortune words - were considered as objects of good fortune.

Thus would the form and content of paintings convey hidden nuances of prosperity messages. Prized paintings were thus valued not merely as works of art. They were deemed superior because of hidden symbolism and their value would increase tenfold. Such paintings were regarded as purveyors of the good fortune *sheng chi* and would hang in places of prominence in the homes of powerful mandarins or warlords. If you possess old valued paintings, first identify the characteristic theme of the painting.

This may be prosperity, longevity, love or any other manifestation of good fortune. Then display it in accordance with the aspirations of the residents. This book contains many themes for you to identify, and many suggestions on how you may want to display good fortune paintings.

> Phonetics & Puns often give clues to hidden meanings of images. Thus a picture of a fish is an expression of abundance because the word for fish *Yu* means abundance. It is for this reason that the Chinese have an almost obsessive passion for keeping fish and why the fish is generally regarded as a good fortune symbol.

This landscape painting has the theme of longevity. There is a grove of pine trees in the foreground. These symbolize long life. This painting has a good meaning and can be hung in the living room preferably on the West wall to benefit the older residents.

To understand symbolism in feng shui, it is vital to appreciate the importance of phonetic sounds in the identification of good fortune symbols. The example of fish is only one of many. The interplay of phonetics and puns offer explanation for why certain creatures and plants are regarded as objects of good fortune. This is why for example, the red bat is considered so auspicious, and why the exchange of mandarin oranges during the lunar New Year is such a popular practice.

According to Chinese belief, anything with the image of the red bat is regarded extremely favourably since the sound for bat also means *great wealth*. It is also believed for instance that when bats fly to your house to nest that they bring good fortune and protection. You should never chase them away. My friend, the owner of an averagely successful travel agency, reported a family of bats came to nest in his home just as the Malaysian Economy went into a tailspin. He welcomed the bats and while competitors were folding up, his agency has thrived so much he is now one of the largest tour operators in Malaysia! As for mandarin oranges, their phonetic sound means *gold*! Receiving oranges is like receiving gold. Puns also explain why the number 8 is regarded so favourably by the Chinese and why the number 4 is so universally disliked. This is because 8 sounds like *to grow* while 4 sounds like *to die*! But do note that the number 4 has auspicious meanings under Flying Star Feng Shui!

The categories of good fortune symbols reflect Man as the cardinal being around which animals, plants and artifacts have meaning. Then there is the unity of heaven and earth. And there are the Deities that symbolize wealth. Even natural phenomenon - clouds, rain, dew, thunder - take on deep symbolic meanings.

Symbols of good fortune that can be used to enhance feng shui can be categorized as celestial creatures of the heavenly realm as well as animals of the earthly realm. Of the celestial creatures, the dragon, the phoenix and the unicorn are said to be legendary and mythical. No one knows for sure if these creatures ever existed in the past. They do not exist today. There are also other legendary creatures whose images are likewise said to bring about happy events, and although they no longer exist, nevertheless they continue to be regarded with favour. The tortoise is the only one of the celestial creatures that still exists today.

Animals as symbols of feng shui are viewed as symbols of protection. Of this category the Fu Dogs are the best known - made famous by the picture of the Fu Dogs in the Forbidden palace complex of Beijing. Tigers, Horses and Elephants - these animals each have specific connotations of good luck.

There are also good fortune plants, auspicious fruits and the special flowers that symbolize love, purity and beauty. Images of these and other symbols of good fortune magnify the effects of correct feng shui orientations and in many instances also speed up the positive impact of feng shui.

The Four Celestial Guardians

East

The celestial Dragon is regarded as the ultimate good luck symbol. His image is generally regarded as auspicious.

Front

Placed in the South, all feathered creatures symbolize the chi of the celestial phoenix.

West

The white tiger of the West is best left alone. Best not to display tiger images.

Back

The tortoise is one of the most auspicious creatures to have in the home or around the garden.

There are eight basic aspirations that make up the components of luck as described in many old feng shui classical texts. These describe the aspirations that matter most in anyone's daily life. To have health and wealth. To gain success at work and attain a high rank both in one's career and socially. To have good descendants luck as well as the luck of powerful patrons and mentors. To have love, romance and a good marriage; and finally to gain wealth and prosperity. These are the things that bring a real feeling of abundance that creates happiness.

There are basic themes to Good Fortune Symbols. These are aspirations that bring happiness - to live a long & healthy life, to attain high social rank and recognition, to have wealth & prosperity, to have successful children and especially to have sons to carry on the family name.

There are symbols that are said to represent all eight of these aspirations and in many cases the types of luck overlap. Of the eight probably the most popular and widely used are the **symbols of longevity,** of which there are many - the most significant being the God of Longevity named **Sau.** His image, is in many Chinese households that have a prominent Patriarch, since long life for the Patriarch is considered of paramount importance. Sau is often depicted as an old man with an elongated forehead,

Sau, the God of Longevity

holding the staff that carries the gourd and in his hand the fruit of immortality the peach. He is also often accompanied by the crane or the deer - both also being symbols of immortality.

Symbols of wealth and financial success are also very popular. There are many different categories of prosperity symbols - some supposedly more potent than others. Perhaps the easiest of the wealth symbols to use would be the different kinds of money, coins and ingots.

Old Chinese coins are extremely popular and also extremely potent in calling upon the luck of both heaven and earth. These square holes in the center of the round coins symbolize the fusion of heaven and earth, bringing prosperity chi which is believed to activate and energize prosperity luck.

The third major category are the **symbols of romance and conjugal happiness.** There are many emblems that signify the happiness of love and marriage and these can be used to enhance the luck of love.

The origins of good fortune symbols are usually legends and myths that have survived the centuries by word of mouth. Rarely are these symbols used in an esoteric or religious sense. Instead they are regarded as emblems that complement the good feng shui of a home; and to express goodwill and friendship in a social sense.

Mandarin Ducks symbolise a happy marriage

it denotes good wishes for a bright career; and so it goes on. There are symbols to suit almost every *hei see* or literally every *happy occasion*.

Naturally such auspicious type gifts would be most inappropriate for those wishing to express condolences at the loss of a member of the family. For such sad yin occasions, symbolism is usually kept to a minimum.

Modern recipients of these kinds of carefully thought out gifts should inspect and study the decorative symbols carefully in order to identify the exact good wishes being conveyed. Usually the accompanying calligraphy on paintings also offers clues to the meaning of the symbolism.

The function of symbols is to bring good luck to households and express good wishes to friends during festive and other happy occasions. Symbols thus play a big role in the giving of gifts. As in the western tradition of bringing flowers to a friend or relative for birthdays, anniversaries and other celebratory occasions. So do the Chinese bring a vase, a painted dish or an embroidered purse - each appropriately decorated with symbols that express the kind of good fortune appropriate to the occasion.

Thus **peaches** and **cranes** are always suitable for birthdays since these express the wish for long life implicit in which is good health; the **double happiness sign** or a pair of **mandarin ducks** would be great as a wedding present; a peony would be excellent for the coming of age of a young daughter; the **jade scepter of authority** would be good as a graduation gift since

The Crane on a Tortoise symbolises longevity

Peaches, the fruits of Immortality

> Bright red or vermilion is the colour that spells good fortune. Gifts wrapped in red symbolize the giving of premium yang energy. Red is also the colour worn and used to decorate symbols that are used during marriages, births and birthday celebrations

The **colour red** is considered to be especially auspicious, and is widely used during the lunar New Year as well as during the celebration of weddings and birthdays. Indeed, the **traditional Chinese bride** is always dressed in red. All three major outfits worn during wedding celebrations should be red in colour and decorated with all kinds of happiness symbolic objects. The three outfits are the **Quah traditional dress** worn at the main ceremony; the dress worn at the wedding dinner party, and the wedding attire worn during the tea giving ceremony to the parents. The decorative symbols can be the double happiness symbol or the dragon phoenix symbol.

The Double Happiness symbol

Dragon & Phoenix

Red is also the dominant colour during **the lunar New Year celebrations**.

For instance, to ensure a good year, the women of the family are expected to wear a new dress made of red materials. The matriarch distributes gifts of cash contained in red packets that have auspicious designs. Red lanterns are lit and hung in front of the main door throughout the 15 days of the New Year, and all fruits and sweetmeats served are placed on a bed of bright red paper. The use of red reflects an unconscious practice of good feng shui because red is symbolic of the auspicious yang *chi* forces which are said to be essential for bringing good fortune into the homes of the living.

Red is not the only good fortune colour. Yellow and purple are the other two auspicious colours. **Yellow** has long been considered an imperial colour associated with the emperors while **purple** is so lucky that it is regarded by many feng shui masters as being even more auspicious than red.

But wrapping paper is seldom plain red or yellow or purple. To transmit positive messages, wrapping paper or containers are always covered with a lucky pattern or auspicious motifs.

The selection of symbols for this book was influenced by their relevance in feng shui. A great deal of importance was also placed on their relevance and the practicality of their use in this modern day and age.

There must be thousands of symbols in the Chinese pantheon but for this book I have selected only those symbols deemed to represent good fortune. I have also used a certain amount of leeway in allowing myself to select only the symbols I like. Thus only those I can recommend with the genuine conviction that I have either used them with a certain amount of success, or at least I have seen them displayed in the homes of wealthy and successful people. Or practitioners of feng shui whom I trust and respect have personally recommended them to me.

Practitioners of feng shui are advised to use this book as a reference guide to ascertain the meanings of Chinese decorative symbols. Select the symbols that appeal to you and take your time inviting them into your home.

There is no need to rush into filling your home with all the suggestions contained in this book. It is better to go slowly. Shop with care. In your enthusiasm do not over pay for a decorative object just because it has a motif or symbol you want. Thus do not purchase a vase with flowers when you do not like the shape of the vase! Nor display a traditional dragon if you feel this

will clash with the modern décor of your home. In using symbols of good fortune, there is always room for good taste and good design.

Chinese symbolism is founded on legendary matter that goes as far back in time as the I Ching. Like feng shui, symbolism has undergone many variations of form, content and interpretation. To make good use of these symbols as a supplement to feng shui, the principles of yin and yang and the five elements must at all times be taken account of.

We have seen that a great deal of symbolic meaning come from the Chinese fondness for playing on the sounds of words, on the mythology of Taoism, on the influences of Buddhism and on the tenets of Confucianism. These combine into a national potpourri of meanings that give symbolism a rich tapestry upon which to paint broad-based manifestations of various types of good fortune. There are variations in the subtle shades of meanings and even the same legend often has different versions in different geographical localities.

But overriding all these localized differences is a pervasive acceptance of all the good fortune icons as vanguards of happiness, wealth and long life. Thus all Chinese accept that **the dragon** is the premier symbol of good fortune, that **the phoenix** is the harbinger of opportunities, that **the peony** is the king of flowers, full of the promise of young love and happiness. These and other well-known, popular symbols are only the tip of the iceberg. The list of auspicious symbols is a long one. But simply knowing the meanings of symbols does not do much to energize the feng shui of a room or home.

The Chinese Dragon is the premier symbol of good fortune

Good fortune symbols should be correctly placed in the home or office for them to fulfill the great promise of their meanings. It is necessary to understand the derivations and basis for them being regarded as good fortune symbols. It is also necessary to understand their yin or yang aspects, and the element family they belong to. There is no simple cook book approach with recipes of good fortune accompanying the symbols.

This is because symbols can be simple and easy to use or they can possess a plethora of feng shui possibilities. Some symbols can bring good fortune whereever they are placed. Others require careful diagnosis of their elements and of their yin or yang nature before deciding their most auspicious spot. There is balance, compatibility and harmony of the intangible *chi* forces to take account of. There is also the question of size, of colours and the material they are made of.

The celestial creatures of the feng shui compass highlights the preliminary set of symbols used in feng shui. Thus the dragon, tiger, phoenix and tortoise make up the first set of creatures that can be energized to bring good fortune to the home.

I have made brief mention of the four celestial creatures that dominate the graphic symbolism of landscape feng shui. In many of the old classical texts on feng shui, the environment that surrounds a home is lyrically described in terms of the dragon and tiger presence to the left and right of the house respectively. It is where there is the presence of these two creatures that good feng shui is believed to be. These creatures are often interpreted to mean hills, mountains and elevated land. It is for this reason that undulating land is always considered to be more auspicious than completely flat land.

Urban dwellers who reside in places where the land is flat and where there is no presence of dragons can however simulate the green dragon by displaying the vibrant image of the **green dragon on the East** wall of the living room. This is believed to successfully create the cosmic *chi* of the dragon inside the home. Paintings of dragons need not be large for them to bring good fortune. Small paintings or even a postcard size print of a Chinese dragon correctly placed along the East wall energizes the precious breath of the dragon. The use of symbolism in feng shui thus starts with the dragon image.

As for **the tiger**, it is not necessary to put an image of the tiger inside the house, although tigers placed outside the home take on protective energies for the residents. But it is extremely beneficial to simulate both the phoenix and the turtle. These two creatures are potent and significant good fortune energizers.

Place the **phoenix in the South**. In feng shui terms, this means either the South of the living room or the South of the home itself or even the South of the land plot. It can be placed inside the home or outside in the garden.

Later in the chapter on this celestial creature, I will discuss substitutes of other feathered creatures that can represent the phoenix. Activating the phoenix brings many different types of luck, the most important of which is the luck of money-making opportunities. Place the **tortoise in the North**. Once again, in feng shui terms, this means either the North of the living room, of the house or of the garden. Find out where North is in your home by using any western compass.

Place a Phoenix in the South

The twelve animals of the Chinese Zodiac symbolize the Earthly Branches. Each of the animals, starting with the Rat and ending with the Boar, has corresponding compass directions. These offer clues on where to place images of these animals thereby magnifying the energy and positive attributes of these animals.

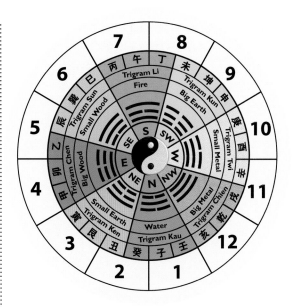

In addition to the four celestial creatures, another set of animals also feature prominently in feng shui practice. These are the twelve animals of the Chinese zodiac - the Rat, the Ox, the Tiger, the Rabbit, the Dragon, the Snake, the Horse, the Sheep, the Monkey, the Dog, the Rooster and the Boar. Each of these animals has a corresponding direction that occupies 30 degrees of the compass angle. Each of the directions occupies two subsections of the main direction. Thus the table here summarizes the twelve animals and their corresponding directions. These directions are represented in the diagram of the compass with the numbers clearly marked out for ease of reference.

Find the animal sign that rules your own birth chart, and then checking from the table below determine the sector of your home which corresponds to your ruling "animal." Then place an image of that animal in the sector of your living room which corresponds to that direction. Thus if you were born in the year of the Rooster, the corresponding direction would be 10, which corresponds to the direction WEST, so placing a ceramic Rooster in the West would be energizing the

#	Animal	Direction
1	Rat	North
2	Ox	N/NE
3	Tiger	E/NE
4	Rabbit	EAST
5	Dragon	E/SE
6	Snake	S/SE
7	Horse	South
8	Sheep	S/SW
9	Monkey	W/SW
10	Rooster	West
11	Dog	W/NW
12	Boar	N/NW

Earthly Branch of your Four Pillars chart. And if you were born in the year of the Tiger then it would be beneficial to place an image of a tiger in the E-NE sector of your living room (which corresponds to direction 3 in the chart). This is a simplified technique of applying symbolic feng shui based on the Four Pillars method. For more on how to use the twelve animals to enhance your feng shui, please refer to chapter 10.

> The symbols of the wu xing categorized under the five elements are symbols that energize, strengthen and magnify the direction that corresponds to the element. Each sector is also identified with a different kind of luck. This is one of the simplest ways of strengthening the elements of corners with good fortune symbols.

There are groupings of symbols that are associated with each of the five elements. This association is based on the theory of *wu xing* or five elements, probably the most significant dimension to the understanding and interpretation of feng shui principles. *Wu xing* is the major principle on which both corrective and activating feng shui is based, and many symbols can be used either for correcting bad feng shui features or for activating good feng shui.

According to *wu xing*, everything in the Universe - even and especially the eight primary and secondary directions of the compass - can be categorized as belonging to either one of the five elements - wood, fire, water, metal and earth. According to the laws of feng shui, these five elements have both a producing and a destroying cycle. When you apply these two major principles of feng shui to your living or work space, you will realize two things:

- One, you will realize that there are a great number of creative and personalized methods for creating good feng shui

- Two, you will understand why I keep saying feng shui can be as easy or as difficult as you want it to be.

Feng shui does not have to be difficult for it to work but it must be based on basic fundamental principles. *Wu xing* is one of these basic fundamentals.

Thus to use the theory of *wu xing* in the practice of symbolic feng shui:

- first learn to identify good fortune objects,

- next, practice categorizing these objects according to the 5 elements correctly.

- and thirdly, try to understand the nature and dimensions of the productive and destructive cycles of the five elements.

The Cycle of Elements

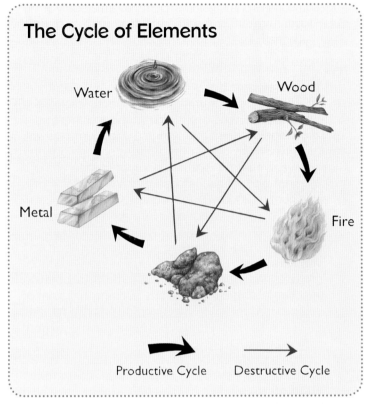

Water

Wood

Metal

Fire

Productive Cycle   Destructive Cycle

Feng shui is based on the correct balance of the two primordial forces Yin and Yang and the use of symbols must always take account of this. In the houses of the living, yang energies are always more meaningful than yin energies, but the two forces act in consonance and objects that have strong symbolic meaning cannot upset this balance.

The other important fundamental principle underlying the correct practice of authentic feng shui is that of Yin and Yang. The symbol of yin and yang eloquently describes the balance of these two opposing primordial forces.

The essence of Yin and Yang energies are diametrically opposite to each other, as can be seen in the simple representation illustrated here. Yin is black and yang is white. Yin is dark and yang is bright. All the other attributes of these two forces are likewise opposite to each other in this fashion. Yet for good feng shui chi to be created in any space, working or living, both of these two forces or their intrinsic chi must not only be present, but they should be in balance.

This does not mean there needs to be equal doses of each type of chi energy. What it does mean is that for **abodes of the living**, what we call yang houses, there should be a lot more *yang energy* to sustain the energy associated with the living. But there should not be so much yang that yin disappears completely. In the same way for yin abodes or the houses of the dead, in feng shui for gravesites and burial grounds, there should be a lot more of yin than yang, but never to the extent that yang disappears completely. The principle therefore is never to have an excess of either yang or yin.

And when there appears to be, you can use symbols to correct the imbalance. Look at the diagram again and you will see that in the yin sector there is a bit of yang and in the yang sector there is a bit of yin.

Symbols of yin and yang are categorized according to their attributes. Thus sun symbols are yang while water symbols are yin. Fire mountains that have sharp triangular peaks are yang, while water mountains that look undulating in appearance are yin. Symbolic feng shui requires you to differentiate clearly between yang objects and yin objects. Develop an instinctive ability to spot if an object is yin or yang before purchasing or displaying it.

First Heaven Sequence

Later Heaven Sequence

Design motifs and patterns can vary according to shapes according to the five elements – fire, wood, water, earth and metal. Each element has a distinctive shape, which can be used for fine-tuning interior decoration feng shui.

The Pa Kua is the eight-sided octagonal symbol of feng shui analysis. Look at the Pa Kuas shown on this page and note the different arrangement of the trigrams in the two Pa Kuas. This different arrangement of the trigrams highlights the fact that in feng shui practice, two types of Pa Kuas are recognized. These are the **Yang Pa Kua** and the **Yin Pa Kua.**

These two types of Pa Kuas have different arrangements of the eight trigrams. Since trigrams represent the root symbols of the I Ching, they are also considered the base symbols of feng shui. Each side or sector of the Pa Kua takes its feng shui meanings from the trigram that is placed there. While it is not necessary to enter into an academic treatise on why there are two different trigram arrangements, it is necessary to understand the nature of these differences, and to know which Pa Kua to use for what purpose.

THE YIN PA KUA shown on the top is mainly used to undertake feng shui analysis of yin dwellings i.e. for gravesite feng shui and in the application of some of the formulas of Flying Star time dimension feng shui. It is also the Pa Kua used as a defensive tool against poison arrows. Note the exact placement of the trigrams. Chien (3 solid lines) is placed South, while Kun (3 broken lines) is placed North. Thus South is the place of **ultimate yang** or Heaven, while North is the place of **ultimate yin** or Earth.

THE YANG PA KUA shown on the right here is the one used exclusively for undertaking feng shui analysis of yang dwellings i.e. houses of the living. Note the placement of each of the eight trigrams has changed positions. Now the 3 solid lines of the trigram Chien which represents the ultimate yang energy has moved to the Northwest, while Kun the 3 broken lines trigram of ultimate yin, matriarchal energy has moved to the Southwest. Carefully study the other trigrams and their respective placements. Note also the element attributes of each of the eight compass directions. Later you will find that many of the recommendations are based on the element associations of the directions.

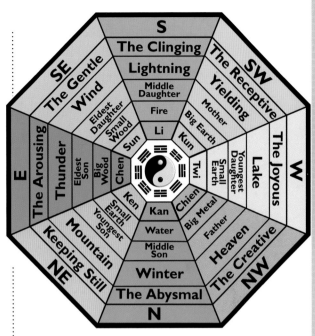

Matching the elements and attributes to each of the compass directions creates the basis for symbolic feng shui. All symbols have chi energies that derive from what they are made of and where they are placed. Understanding this can help create maximum benefits out of their display and usage.

The Pa Kua symbol reproduced here reveal the layers of symbolic meanings applicable in each of the eight sectors. These offer clues on how many of the traditional symbols of good fortune can be made to enhance home décor. For instance, if you wish to energize the EAST sector of your home, note this is the place of the trigram *Chen* which represents the eldest son, big wood, yang energy, thunder and all the feelings associated with arousing. Thus things made of wood are suitable. All colours associated with this element are also suitable. Thus greens and browns would enhance this part of the house. In addition, the shape associated with the wood element is rectangular, so this shape is good for this corner. In terms of celestial creatures, the East is the place of the dragon. Male and yang energies in this corner are strong. If they are in excess, cool down excessive yang with water, an element that is also in harmony with the wood element. If the East corner is missing, then all attributes associated with this location are deemed to be missing.

When practicing symbolic feng shui, try to work out the attributes of each of the sector directions paying particular attention to the element of each sector. Just making sure that the element of the sector is properly energized is already a significant part of feng shui. Thus when you place an auspicious symbol in any corner, try to use an image that is in harmony with the element of the sector. This requires knowledge of the destructive and productive cycles of the elements. Do not place a symbol whose element clashes with the element of the corner.

> ## Patterns and motifs that reflect the five elements can strengthen the energy of these elements when used correctly. The matching of element with pattern or design is one of the easiest and most effective ways of magnifying the positive energies of the sectors of your living and workspace. The sectors are identified according to the elements.

Shown on this page are four frequently used patterns that appear in wallpaper prints; on curtains and as tile designs. By understanding the element association of design motifs, it is possible to work them into interior decoration ideas. The sample examination here will give practitioners the basis on which feng shui analysis is undertaken. Thus consider:

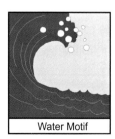

Water Motif

The water motif here is generic. It looks like a sea wave and the bubbles indicate yang water i.e. water that has life. This design would be excellent for any corner that benefits from water. This

means North, Southeast and East. This motif is great in black and blue and is ideal for restaurants, wine bars and pubs.

The Square Maze

The square maze design indicated here suggests the element of earth since the square symbol stands for earth. It is ideally suitable for the earth corners of the home, which are the Southwest and the Northeast. It is also excellent for rooms located at the heart of the home. A square motif is also suited for industries and business engaged in property and real estate.

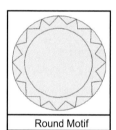

Round Motif

The round motif shown here is suitable for the metallic corners of the home. These are the corners that lie in the West or Northwest part of the house. The pattern also denotes a precious stone, which has an auspicious meaning since precious stones are akin to metal, being mined from mother earth; this symbol is thus considered auspicious in metal corners.

Mountain Range

The mountain range shown here is suggestive of support for the house. Placed in the back half of the home, it creates protection chi. But it also suggests big earth, so something like this when placed in the SW corner of the home would create chi that is beneficial to the mother, as well as enhance all family and sibling relationships.

Chapter One:
Symbols of Wealth & Success

Make liberal use of good fortune **coins** and **ingots** to enhance and attract the chi of wealth to all your business ventures. Simulate the **merchant ship** laden with cargo bringing wealth into your home; learn to create **wealth vases**, bowls and wallets.

Keep **three legged toads**, **bats** and **arowanas** to activate the yang of prosperity. Create a **goldfish** paradise and use the most magnificent symbol of all - the mighty and celestial **dragon,** its mate the **phoenix** and all the other creatures of good fortune - the **chi lin (the dragon horse)**, the **dragon tortoise** - frolicking with precious

pearls and **pots of gold** underneath a **crystal rainbow**. Learn all about the wealth significance of lesser known symbols of good fortune like the **precious horse** and the other auspicious creatures of the Chinese pantheon - the **pi chen**, the **pi yao**, and the **gold spouting mongoose**. Find out how to display the **wish fulfilling gem tree** and the **wish granting cow**. Place these and other symbols of prosperity in a feng shui orientation and bring wealth energy into your home.

Authentic Good Fortune Coins

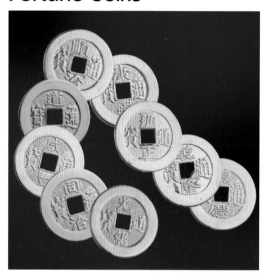

These Chinese coins represent the powerful union of heaven and earth. Described as being "square within and round without", these round coins, usually made of copper, have been used as metal currency from the T'ai Kung in the 11th century BC. The square shape in the center is the energy of the earth, while the circle represents the chi of heaven. Combined, they drive the power of wealth luck, and when energized with red or gold string, yang energy breathes precious life into them, transforming them into powerful emblems of wealth and prosperity. Naturally, coins taken from a rich man's home would possess an abundance of wealth energy, and the *nine emperor coins* that represent the reign of nine emperors of a single dynasty denote continued wealth for nine generations.

Those keen to do so may spend some time "treasure hunting" for authentic antique coins from the various Chinese dynasties. The Chinese characters on the coins usually bear the name of the reign. When you have collected coins from nine emperors reigns, tie them together with a red thread and hang them on the wall behind you at work. This means you have the financial support of nine emperors and is believed to be most auspicious. I believe that these coins should ideally be chosen from the reign periods that represent periods of prosperity. Thus, coins from the Emperor Chien Lung's period or from the Kang Hsi period will be better than from the closing days of the Ching Dynasty. The **wu chu** or tael coin of the Han Dynasty (206 BC to AD25) is considered to be one of the most lucky and decorative objects of prosperity. The *wu chu* coin has been reproduced in gold, silver, bronze and jade and worn around the neck on a chain or chord for a long time, but the genuine *wu chu* coin is very rare. A sketch of this and other dynastic lucky coins are shown below.

Wu Chu coin

Tang Dynasty coin

Kang Hsi coin

Yang & Yin sides

According to Chinese scholars, some of the old antique coins were believed to be so powerful in attracting wealth luck, families would let their sons wear these coins round their necks as good luck amulets. The provincial coins of the Kang Hsi period, for example, bearing characters on yang and yin sides as shown in the previous page, are believed to have talismanic powers when strung together with red thread or hung round the neck with a gold chain. Coins of the Chien Lung period are also held in high esteem.

For feng shui purposes, some of the provincial cities of China were said to have deities of wealth at the city gates, and hung around the neck of these deities of wealth would be nine coins strung together with red thread.

For modern day usage of these good fortune coins, the gold and diamond equivalent of the coins would be a suitable substitute. The use of genuine precious materials like gold and diamonds would bring the ultimate chi energy to the coins, and in addition to the pendant and ring shown here, it is also possible to wear earrings, cufflinks and tie pins all fashioned with these diamond and gold copies of this once old symbol.

The ideal number of coins to wear on the body would be nine coins, thus a ring with a pair of earrings with three coins each (as shown) would be ideal, or a necklace with a pair of earrings.

Coins Worn As Protective Amulets

Apart from bringing prosperity, these good fortune coins were also used as protective amulets. Thus **nine coins taken from the Chien Lung period** (either the genuine old coins or gold/jade imitations will be acceptable) are to be tied with red string and hung around the neck of a Deity of Wealth for 7, 14 or 21 days.

This would symbolically empower the coins with the Deity's chi and thus acquire virtue. The coins are then to be worn around the neck of the child to overcome the **30 dangerous barriers of a person's life**. The number of coins to be hung around the neck would be equal to how old the child is (in Chinese statement of age, please add one year); and each year, a fresh coin would be added during the first day of the lunar New Year until the child attains the age of 15. By that time, the child is believed to have symbolically and successfully crossed all the **barriers along the path of life**.

These barriers are those of the 4 seasons, the 4 pillars, the demon cow king; the devils gate demon; the insurmountable difficulties; the golden hen falling into a well; and the barrier of the private parts.

Then there are the barriers of the hundred days; the broken bridge; the nimble foot; the five genii; the golden padlock; the iron snake; the bathing tub; the white tiger; and the Buddhist monks.

Then there are the barriers posed by the heavenly dog; that invoking heaven's pity; and those associated with the lock and key; where the bowels are sundered; and where the head is broken. This creates the barriers of the thousand days; of the nocturnal weeping; of the burning broth; of the time when children are buried; where life is shortened; caused by the general's dagger; caused by deep running water or caused by fire and water.

Over time, the use of these coins/amulets became something superstitious to do, and the coins worn around the neck evolved into clusters of coins tied to resemble **swords**, decorated with knots and tassels. Coins used for warding off shar chi or killing breath are known as *Pi Hsieh Chien*.

These knife coins (whose origin go back to the 1st century AD) are believed to make excellent antidotes for feng shui afflicted corners which threaten the loss of wealth of the family. Place them in the corners of your home that give you problems!

Coins to enhance your feng shui

Hang Two Coins Tied with Red Thread Over Shop Door

This will attract wealth to the establishment. The potency of this symbol is said to equal that of the God of Riches. Place the coin directly above the main entrance door. Refresh these coins each year on the first day of the lunar New Year. It is believed

that for this purpose, the genuine Chien Lung Ching Dynasty coins are said to be extraordinarily potent.

> ## Stick Three Coins Tied with Red Thread onto Your Important Files And Invoice Books to Increase Your Business.

Since it can be difficult to find genuine antique Chinese coins, the cottage entrepreneurs of China and Taiwan have now come out with really good copies of Ching Dynasty coins, some of which even look like real gold! If you find an inexpensive source, do like I do and buy a couple of hundred. Usually, they cost about a dollar for three.

These coins are not expensive, just hard to find, and it is this that caused them to be expensive. In the past three years, they have come down in price. I advise buying lots of these coins, as they are so useful.

Stick them onto all your important files; stick them on your cash boxes, in your safe, on your order books and inside your pocket book or wallet.

The physical presence of three coins made energetic with the addition of red or gold thread is said to attract wealth luck wherever they are placed. I have them on my doorknobs, stuck to my fax machine and computer. This brings loads of wonderful opportunities communicated to me by fax and email!

I keep lots of coins in my home, all tied with red or gold thread, so I always have stock to give to someone who needs them. This has been one of the most simple and most effective feng shui tips, one that has benefited so many people!

It is not necessary for the coins to be genuinely old. The power of the coins comes from its shapes and meanings, not from its age.

Note that when you stick coins on your files and fax machines and so forth, the **yang** side must be up as shown here. The **yang** side is always the side with the four Chinese characters. The side with two characters is the yin side.

Coins to enhance the wealth of a marriage

In the *Imperial Record of Chinese Coins*, it was recorded that there is a certain form of coin shaped talisman known as "coins for throwing into the bed chamber" which would not only bring great wealth to the couple but also plenty of successful children.

The story here is that one of the emperors of the Tang Dynasty who was advised to do so by his feng shui adviser had coins fashioned of gold and silver thrown onto the marriage bed of his favourite daughter. These gold coins were engraved with various auspicious phrases.

To strengthen the luck of young married couples therefore, one can take a leaf out of these Imperial records. In the old days, emperors had access to the best feng shui brains of the country. It is also

reported, for example, that the Emperor Wu of the Han Dynasty and his consort were very superstitious so they arranged to be showered with gold and silver coins each time they rested on the royal couch.

This was based on the belief that the coins would bring lots of descendants luck to the Dynasty and bless them with many sons.

Thus coins were used not only to attract riches, but also to ward off killing energy and to ensure the dynastic continuance of a family's name.

A very popular good fortune symbol favoured by Chinese mothers is a round disk-like **jade pendant** with a square hole in the center. This is worn around the neck for good luck and protection. It is believed that the soft smoothness of jade combined with the coin shape are extremely auspicious. A variation of this is the ten jade coins tied together with red thread. This is similar to the ten emperor coins.

Shown on the right here are the **ten emperor coins**; and shown on the left here are the **8 jade disks**. Both of these are symbols of good fortune used by different feng shui masters to encourage the flow of positive chi. Hang the ten emperor coins at work behind your chair. (I prefer to have nine instead of ten coins). Hang the 8 pieces of jade in your bedroom to enhance descendants luck.

Enhancing Luck by Combining with Other Symbols of Good Fortune.

Good fortune coins are combined with almost all the animal symbols of good fortune. Combined with the bat, the meaning is "good fortune now!" Combined with two magpies, the meaning is "may one see good fortune before one's eyes"; and combined with the cow, the chi lin, the sheep, the mongoose, the tortoise, or the dragon, the connotations of wealth and success are multiplied a thousand times over. These animals are shown sitting or standing on a bed of coins, itself a representation of abundance and plenty.

Gold ingots on a merchant ship

One of the most popular **symbols of business success** leading to the accumulation of wealth that was favoured by the Chinese merchant traders in South East Asia during the turn of the century was the merchant ship. Many used sailing ships laden with cargo as their business logo, with great success.

Sailing ship
laden with gold

You can create a symbolic wealth ship piled high with gold ingots to attract higher income and success to your business. These gold ingots need not be real. Get a dozen imitation gold ingots from Chinatown and go searching for a merchant sailing ship. Make sure the ship you display does not have cannons. Ships with cannons are war ships, not sailing ships, and cause more harm than good by shooting cannons at you. Your ship can be made of wood, jade, metal; it can be gold plated, or even made of gold if you can afford! Fill the model ships with ingots or crystals that look like diamonds. Let the cargo overflow onto the deck.

Next, place the model ship inside the office, preferably in the foyer area. Position the ship correctly, since it must look like it is sailing IN and not sailing out. Check that this is so, by looking at the sails. If the ship is sailing outwards, you will lose money. Let it seem like the wind is strongly blowing the ship into harbour. For it to have really good meaning, the ship must be laden with gold and jewels, and must *never* be empty.

Wherever the ship is placed, there will be the harbour! Let your office be the harbour. Or you can also place a ship in your house, preferably on a low table. If you are greedy, you can have more than one ship and make your house into a real "harbour." Each ship represents one source of income! Many ships mean you have many sources of income!

You can also position the ship such that it is **sailing in from your best and most auspicious direction**. You can check this based on your KUA number. (Please refer to my other books PERSONALIZED TIPS or BASIC FENG SHUI.)

Creating a wealth vase

Vases are exceptionally auspicious symbols to have around the house since they signify "perpetual peace and harmony in the home." This is because the phonetic sound of the vase is *ping,* which also means peace. The vase is also one of the eight auspicious signs of Buddhism being one of the objects found on the footprints of Buddha.

To create a **wealth vase**, you can choose from those made of porcelain, crystal, earthenware or of a metal substance like bronze, silver or even gold if you can afford it. The vases shown here is suitable for making a wealth vase. It has a fairly wide mouth and a slender neck, with a wide bottom. This symbolizes plenty of wealth flowing in and once it flows down the narrow neck, stays inside the large base of the vase signifying that wealth will stay in the family for a long long time. If you like, you can shop around for a vase with an even slimmer neck.

If the vase is decorated with auspicious wealth symbols such as the dragon, or the red bat, it is even better. A vase that has the four season flowers will signify that your family will have wealth and harmony through the four seasons of the year (i.e. at all times). A vase decorated with dragons and phoenixes benefits the whole family.

To create the **treasure vase** (referred to as the *pao ping* or rare vase) fill the vase to its brim with the following objects and keep hidden from view:

Wealth vase

- Seven types of semi precious stones. Choose from crystals, corals, and other semi precious stones like lapis, pearl, jasper, cornelian, quartz, tiger eye, aquamarine, topaz, amethyst, citrine and malachite.

- A bit of soil from a rich man's house. You will have to be ingenious about this. Don't steal. Ask for it. Soil that is given to you is very lucky.

- A red packet filled with real money, preferably a hundred dollar note.

- Three, six or nine Chinese coins tied with red thread (optional).

- Five types of *"nourishing fruits"* to signify plenty to eat at all times. Some say this also guarantees good descendants luck. This can be millet, dates, wheat, barley, sorghum, red beans, green beans, or soya beans. Place in a small plastic bag. (This too is optional)

The legend of the three legged toad

The three legged toad is probably the most auspicious symbol of money-making. There are a couple of myths associated with the origins of this belief. In fact, according to Chinese mythology, the three legged toad is said to exist only on the moon, which it succeeds in swallowing during an eclipse. As a result, it is sometimes said to signify the unattainable. An extension of this myth is that the wife of one of the Eight Immortals stole the elixir of immortality from the Queen of the West, *Hsi Wang Mu*. She fled to the moon where she was turned into a toad! But having tasted the elixir, she had attained immortality and in the midst of being changed into a toad, she had begged for mercy. The Gods, ever compassionate, softened, so that only the upper half of the body took the form of the ugly creature. Instead of the hind quarters, the Gods allowed the retention of the tail of the tadpole. Thus did she become the three legged toad.

In a related legend, the mythical three legged toad is being baited with gold coins by Lui Hai, one of the 8 Immortals, a Minister of State who lived during the tenth century AD. Lui Hai was believed to be proficient in Taoist magic and had knowledge of the toad's powers for attracting wealth and prosperity.

After much searching for this mythical creature, Lui Hai found it hiding deep inside a well. Aware of the toad's fondness for money, he is said to have baited the creature to come up from a well.

As bait, he used a red line tied with gold coins. This has resulted in the painting of a child baiting the three legged frog with coins tied on a long red string to become itself an emblem meaning that "wealth is about to come".

The legend of the three legged toad as an auspicious symbol of wealth thus originated from the popular representation of Lui Hai, who is shown with one foot resting on the toad and holding in his hand a red string on which five gold coins are strung. This image was said to be most auspicious and conducive to attracting great good fortune. Since then, the three legged toad with a coin in its mouth has become the symbol for attracting wealth and prosperity.

Over time, the legend grew and today, decorative representations of the three-legged toad show it sitting on a bed of coins and ingots and always with a coin in its mouth. Lui Hai the Immortal has mysteriously vanished from the image!

The three legged toad in feng shui

The Chinese do not distinguish very clearly between the frog and the toad. But they do believe that the spawn of the frog falls

from heaven, like dew, and that the spittle-like white juice from the toad can be used very effectively as medicine for all kinds of forehead, throat and heart ailments. Infirmities associated with these three upper chakra centers of the body are believed to be hard to cure, and a dried version of the toad's spittle is said to be a good cure. This can be bought from Chinese Medicine shops. It is also very good medicine for those who smoke too much!

Where to place the toad ?

There seem to be conflicting advice being given on the best position, location and orientation of the toad for it to be most beneficial. I myself place the three legged toad near the vicinity of my main front door. They are placed fairly low, but not on the ground. Coffee table level is about right.

I do not recommend placing the toad directly in front of the door. The best place would be one of the corners diagonal to the door. And then the toad should be looking at the door as though expecting to greet in the wealth chi. There are those who say that the toad should face the door during the daylight hours and be turned to face inwards during the night time hours. I do not see the need to do this.

Also, you can place as many three legged toads in your house or office as you wish. I myself have them all over my living room, dining room and also in my garden, hidden between rocks near my small fish ponds and waterfall garden. But the total number of toads in my house never exceeds nine. If you are like me and wish to have these toads all around your house, do be discreet in your display of them and

do keep them in the public areas of your home. In other words, do not keep them in bedrooms and kitchens.

Fish in water combines two of the most powerful symbols of abundance

The fish is the most popular emblem of wealth because the Chinese character for fish, *yu* (shown here), also means abundance. During the lunar New Year, the word *sarng* is added to it to imply growth in abundance. The exchange of gifts of live fish indicates the significant goodwill of friends and relatives.

If you wish to activate the good fortune symbolism of fish in water, it is best to consider keeping some of the more popular of the good fortune fish. These are the carp, the goldfish and the arowana, but essentially, any brightly coloured or red fish are believed to be signs of good fortune.

If you are thinking of keeping an aquarium of arowanas, a pond of carps or a bowl of goldfish, here are some useful tips to help you make the best of your water feature:

- Place your water feature in the Southeast, East or North of your home, your apartment or your garden. Do not do so if these sectors happen to fall into one of your bedrooms, since water in the bedroom cause losses and is not recommended.

- Always keep the water well oxygenated and clean since this generates the precious and wealth bringing yang energy that you want. It also ensures your fish are healthy.

- If any of your fish die for no apparent reason, give all the remaining fish a bath of appropriate medicine and then replace with new ones. Do not worry about fish dying, but say a silent prayer for its departed soul for it too was once a living being. Fish that die are believed to have helped you avoid some specific misfortune.

- Make sure your water feature is neither too large nor too small. Balance is vital. If it is too small it might not be as effective and if it is too large, the excess of water could cause problems. Too much water drowns you.

- In terms of number of fish to keep, multiples of 9 are a good guide. But if you are keeping arowanas, a single arowana in the North sector is the most potent. If you want to keep more, 5 is a good number to keep, since, in addition to generating good wealth feng shui, the arowana is also a symbol of protection.

- Make sure you do not mix your fish. The arowana for instance will devour all other fish. The goldfish will have its beautiful tail fins destroyed by the carp, and the carp and the arowana simply cannot coexist together.

Arowana or Dragon Fish

The Arowana or dragon fish for excellent wealth feng shui

In recent years, the tropical arowana or dragon fish has become increasingly popular as a powerful feng shui energizer of wealth luck. This exceptionally beautiful fish comes in many different varieties. The shape and colour of the arowana varies according to where they originate, and it is only those varieties that show a tinge of pink, gold or silver that are the prized specimens with good feng shui connotations. If the fish does not show scales that have the silvery sheen, they are regarded as poor relations to the real thing. Thus, those wishing to keep the arowana should be careful. The fish is also expensive, both to buy and to maintain, since they generally feed on live fish, prawns or worms.

I kept five arowanas in the late Eighties to capture much needed prosperity luck for myself and after the fish had brought me the fortune I needed to retire from corporate life and released them into the Stanley reservoir of Hong Kong. But I have since felt great regret at having fed them a diet of live goldfish. If I were to keep them again, I would train them to eat special fish pellets. This is not easy to do, since arowanas are very fussy in their diet.

But I do urge you to try, since feeding them live bait is not good for one's karma. I have now changed to keeping goldfish instead. Another alternative is to keep the image of the arowana in gold or dark maroon. Display the arowana in the wealth corner of the living room, (the Southeast corner) or the corner diagonal to the front door.

The gold fish is the all-time favorite for excellent wealth feng shui

The two words that mean gold fish are also the two words that phonetically mean gold and abundance. The word *kum* is 'gold' and the word *yu* means 'fish' as well as 'abundance'. Thus *kum yu* means gold in abundance. For this reason, the Chinese have always been very fond of keeping goldfish.

To use goldfish to enhance your wealth feng shui, go for the varieties that look fat and prosperous and are red or gold in colour. Thus, the specially developed Japanese

ryukins which are a bright red are an excellent choice. The *lion headed* Chinese varieties that have white silver scales and a bright red head are also excellent. Keep eight of these yang coloured fish together with a single one of the black variety. Choose a black goldfish that swims vigorously and is completely black with no other markings. This combination of 8 yang coloured fish with one yin coloured fish will ensure not just prosperity but also protection against loss and being cheated. The total number of 9 represents the fullness of heaven and earth.

Keep your goldfish in an aquarium, or better yet, in a goldfish bowl so that you look down into the fish from the top. If you place oxygenators into the water, the bubbles in the water keep it energized with yang energy. It is also a good idea to have a filter to ensure the water stays clean.

Place this auspicious water feature in the North part of your home or garden for maximum good luck. Or place it in the East or Southeast. Do not place live goldfish in water in the South part of your home. In the South, goldfish do more harm than good. If you wish to keep more than nine goldfish, you should keep them in multiples of nine.

Almost all varieties of auspiciously coloured fish are good feng shui

The fish has always been an emblem of wealth and abundance, not just because of the phonetics of the word **yu**, but also because fish are always in such plentiful

supply. Due to their awesome reproductive powers, they are also a symbol of fertility, and because they swim happily in their own environment, they have become an emblem of connubial bliss and harmony. In the old days, fish were almost always included as one of the items in the betrothal gifts given to the parents of the bride. This was due to its auspicious significance. In addition, a pair of fish was also noted for being emblematic of the joys of union, particularly of a sexual nature. The fish emblem was also believed to be a charm against bad luck, since it is included among the auspicious signs on the footprints of the Buddha.

The **double fish symbol**, shown in the sketch here, is regarded as one of the eight Buddhist treasures and is usually embroidered onto door curtains and pillow cases for good luck. The double fish symbol is both an amulet said to possess strong protective energies, as well as an enhancer of good *sheng chi*, worn to attract good luck. In Thailand, children are often given the double fish symbol to wear around their necks. These are usually made of gold, and sometimes set with precious stones like rubies, sapphires and emeralds. Modern day jewellery designs of the double fish symbol set with diamonds and gold are also worn by superstitious rich ladies who believe that the double fish symbol protects

them from being cast aside by their husbands for younger women!

The carp is also a good fortune symbol, suggestive of martial attributes. The carp is known for its legendary valour in swimming against the current to reach the Dragon Gate (*the lung men*) and thus becoming a dragon. The carp is therefore a symbol of perseverance.

The story of the sturgeons of the yellow river making the ascent of the stream during the third moon of each year to attempt passing above the rapids of the *lung men* thereby getting transformed into dragons has become the legend of the dragon carp. It has made the carp the symbol of literary and educational success.

Thus, if you wish your sons or daughters to excel in their examinations and become straight "A" students, keep lots of carp in a pond inside the house. The carp seldom fails to deliver!

The Dragon & Phoenix are multi-tiered symbols of success and prosperity

The Dragon and Phoenix are the ultimate yang and yin symbols of Chinese cosmology and mythology. The **Dragon** is the symbol of male vigour and fertility. The **Phoenix** symbolizes yin splendour and female beauty when placed with the dragon. Alone however, the phoenix takes on yang characteristics and male essence, thereby symbolizing other attributes. Together, the

The Yin Phoenix &
The Yang Dragon

benefits the health of the family. Hung on the South wall, it brings opportunities and recognition for the family.

Place the Dragon in the East to generate an accumulation of cosmic chi

The Dragon is said to be the most potent symbol of good fortune in the Chinese pantheon of symbols. As one of the four creatures of the world's directions and as the principle symbol of feng shui, the dragon stands for new beginnings. It is the standard bearer of the East, the place where the sun rises and where the spring rains originate. The dragon is the powerful emblem of rain, which brings water to the land. Thus the dragon is said to signify the *good water*, which in turn is symbolic of wealth. It is also itself a symbol of continuing success, great attainments and prosperity. Because of this, there are no other symbols that can surpass it in popularity. As a result, Chinese businesses often incorporate the Dragon into their company logo with long-lasting and great success.

Many businesses benefit from the use of the dragon symbol to create the precious cosmic chi. It is this same chi that brings good fortune to houses that enjoy

dragon and phoenix symbolize the emperor and empress.

The presence of the dragon and phoenix together in any home always symbolizes a fruitful marriage blessed with a great deal of success and prosperity as well as many male offspring. This is the principle reason behind it being such a popular symbol for marriage celebrations and especially during the tea drinking ceremony.

The union of these two symbolic creatures at wedding festivities suggests a union blessed with plentiful money and descendants luck. It denotes the beginning of the dynastic family with the Dragon signifying the Patriarch and the Phoenix signifying the Matriarch. Hung as a painting on the NW wall, it favours the patriarch's luck. Hung on the SW wall, it favours the matriarch's luck. Hung on the East wall, it good feng shui. Thus, simulating the dragon inside the home energizes the luck of the dragon.

Where to place the dragon

Place the dragon image in the living room of the home. Get ceramic, porcelain or crystal dragons for the SW and NE corners of the room, and have wooden carved dragons for the East and Southeast. In feng shui, the dragon will be beneficial wherever he is displayed. But to ensure it blends in well with the elements, note the locations given. Also make certain the dragon is not too large as to overwhelm the energies of the home. Usually, it is better to err on the side of it being too small than being too large. The best replicas of dragon are those painted green or made from a green coloured semi precious stone.

Examples of good mediums are aventurine and jade, but since these are expensive, carved wooden dragons are

also effective in simulating the presence of the dragon. But, place the dragon at eye level. It should never be placed too high, since this gets it out of control.

Remember that you are in charge, not the dragon!

Invoke the power of the Nine Dragons

The mainland overlooking Hong Kong is called **Kowloon** which means *nine dragons*, and feng shui masters are always quick to point to the prosperity of this *abode of the nine mighty dragons*. The potency of the nine dragons is given prominence and manifested by the presence of an exceptionally grand Nine Dragon ceramic wall placed in the Forbidden City in Beijing. This screen is brick-faced with a marvelous design of glazed coloured tiles set in the form of nine coiling dragons. They are exceptionally beautiful and look very alive, seemingly ready to fend off all attacks by spirits and negative killing breath. This screen symbolizes all dragons in existence and is thus a protective screen. Later, an exact replica was built and placed in Heibei Park in the city.

In the mid-Eighties, when Hong Kong was going through the throes of nervousness arising from the impending handover to China, a third nine dragon

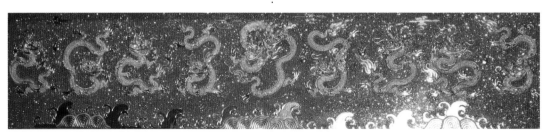

screen was erected on Hong Kong island to face the harbour and Kowloon. These colourful ceramic screens were all placed to tap the tremendous good fortune and protection associated with the nine dragons, each of whom had particular protective attributes. The nine dragons are:

1. **P'u-lao,** who alerts and protects when there is danger. He is the dragon carved on bells, gongs and singing bowls.
2. **Ch'iu-niu,** who creates yang energy with music.
3. **Pi-hsi,** who brings the luck of knowledge and education.
4. **Pa-hsia,** who brings support and strength.
5. **Chao-feng,** who guards temples and other holy places.
6. **Chih wen,** who symbolizes the power of water over fire.
7. **Suan-ni,** who protects from loss and betrayals.
8. **Yai-Tzu,** who protects from physical harm.
9. **Pi-Kau,** who protects against litigation.

If you can obtain a photograph or print of the nine dragon ceramic screen described here, hanging it near the vicinity of the front door invokes the good chi of the nine dragons that benefit and protect all residents of the house. This is irrespective of compass directions since the nine dragons represent the fullness of both heaven and earth, and by implication, all the eight directions.

Energize with the image of the Dragon

The dragon is more than just a symbol of vigilance and safeguard. It is also the ultimate symbol of success. Its image connotes courage and bravery, and the most powerful of all the dragons are the *heaven dragons,* said to bring powerful success luck for the family patriarch. These should be differentiated from the *earth dragons* associated with feng shui. The image of the dragon brings auspicious luck into the home and office. Its image can be placed in any one of the cardinal directions, because although it is affiliated with the East, the dragon is also linked to all four of the cardinal directions. Having said this, the dragon is most powerful in the East, so I strongly recommend you decorate the East wall of your living room with images of the dragon.

The lunar new year is a particularly good time to energize dragon symbolism to attract good fortune and prosperity for the rest of the year. Welcome in the new year with auspicious dragon dances and loud yang energy. To enhance the yang energies of your home, invest in ceramics and porcelain ware that carry the dragon image. Or display the dragon image carrying the pearl and made of semi precious stone. Energize the corners of the living or dining rooms rather than the sleeping quarters.

Improve opportunity luck with the celestial Phoenix

The Phoenix is one of the four celestial creatures of feng shui and the king of all the winged creatures. This magnificent and legendary bird is analogous with good fortune associated with opportunity luck. The phoenix symbolizes resilience - rising from the ashes of loss and destitution to soar to great heights of success and prosperity.

The phoenix is known to bring amazing turnaround luck. Just when you think that all is lost, it opens new channels and opportunities in your work and career. The phoenix on its own is a soaring *yang* symbol. It is associated with the fiery energies of the South, and is also the God of the four winds. Its place in the practice of feng shui is especially potent for those wanting to magnify their chances of success in all fields of endeavour.

If you place the phoenix image in your home, look for a high place - a shelf or cupboard - where it can stand in splendor, its body evoking the five human qualities that attract the good cosmic *chi*. Its head signifies *virtue*; its wings signify a sense of *duty and responsibility*; its back stands for

correct behaviour; its breast spells humanity and *compassion* and its stomach indicates *reliability*. These five qualities are also reflected in the five colours of its feathers.

Place the phoenix image along the South wall or corner of your home or living room. If you cannot find an image of the phoenix, you can use any of the other beautifully feathered birds as substitutes (the peacock or the rooster) but the phoenix will be best. Energizing the phoenix can also be done with porcelain ware and paintings.

I have a crystal phoenix with specks of gold in its body. This was a limited edition piece I received as a gift almost fifteen years ago. I placed it in the South corner of my office when I first received it and it brought me tons of opportunities almost on a continuous basis. Today, I have "retired" it, since I cannot cope with too many opportunities! I have placed it in the SW of the family room to stimulate good harmonious luck for the family.

The Phoenix symbolizes peace and prosperity

The Phoenix presence is always associated with times of peace and prosperity and having the spirit of the phoenix in the home encourages the inflow of harmonious and prosperous chi. This celestial creature presides over the Southern quadrant of the heavens, and in accordance with the fire trigram of the South, is associated with the sun, the warmth of summer and the happiness that comes from a good harvest.

Ultimately, the phoenix brings prosperity, and hence is often drawn gazing into a ball of fire. It is therefore strongly associated with yang energies of the living. But this is only when it is displayed on its own.

When the **phoenix is shown with the dragon**, it takes on its yin aspect, and the joint symbol signifies marital happiness. A picture with the phoenix on the right and the dragon on the left (see diagram above) symbolizes man and wife. Place this in the SW corner of your bedroom if you are desperate to find a mate!

Two phoenixes together also signify connubial intercourse, but the connotations of such a representation refer more to homosexuality, described in the old texts as *false male and empty female phoenix*. Displaying two phoenixes together is thus not encouraged.

Dragon & Phoenix

A **phoenix drawn with a peony** represents young lovers. Sometimes this symbolism is depicted showing children carrying a vase with flowers and sitting on the back of the phoenix.

For wealth, it is recommended that a **cinnabar-coloured phoenix** should be placed high along the South wall. Such a symbol of wealth should be specially commissioned so that it is shown in all its magnificence.

Remember that the phoenix is entirely an imaginary creature. Its elegant stature and attributes can be embellished with every benevolent quality. It should thus be made perfectly beautiful.

The Chi Lin brings prosperity and illustrious sons!

The mythical **Chi Lin** is the Chinese Unicorn, sometimes referred to as the *Dragon Horse*. It is a fabulous creature of good omen, prosperity, success, longevity, illustrious offspring and enchantment. The chi lin brings sons! Supposedly endowed with magical qualities, it is also associated with the *hou tu* square - symbol of numbers used in advanced feng shui analysis. Moreover, it is said to have emerged from the Yellow River bearing on its back the mystical map from which the legendary Fu Hsi (the founder of the I Ching) is said to have devised the written characters of the Chinese language. There are many legends and stories associated with the Chi Lin, almost all praising its many qualities: its perfect goodwill, benevolence and gentle nature.

Chi Lin with 4 scholastic objects brings education luck

The Chi Lin's presence is said to attract the powerful cosmic breath of the dragon, thereby bringing good fortune luck to those residing in the abode. Shown above is a model image of the chi lin which can be found in most Chinese arts and crafts shop. Place this image on your desk to simulate all the good attributes of this magnificent creature. Since it is also regarded as a happy portent, the chi lin is believed to be an auspicious symbol to display at the work place.

The Chi Lin is believed to represent good fortune in promotions for those wanting advancement in their careers, and is especially lucky for those who work in the military. The chi lin is the symbol of the first rank military official, and its image is often embroidered onto court robes as shown here.

The symbolism of the Dragon Tortoise

This legendary symbol combines the powers and attributes of the dragon and the tortoise. These are two of the four spiritually endowed creatures of Chinese symbolism. The image is of a creature with the body of a tortoise and the head of the dragon sitting on a bed of coins and gold ingots. In its mouth is the symbolic coin of prosperity. Like the chi lin, this is a creature of the imagination and demonstrates the way the Chinese use symbolism to enhance the physical space of their living environment. If you look at the picture, you will note there are multiple meanings to the image. Thus:

- The tortoise symbolizes longevity. Here is a creature that is reputed to be able to live to 3000 years without food or air.

- The dragon symbolizes success, courage and determination. That the tortoise has transformed into a dragon indicates impending good fortune in one's career and business endeavours.

- The base of gold ingots upon which the creature sits signifies tremendous wealth and prosperity.

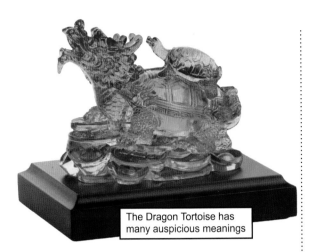

The Dragon Tortoise has many auspicious meanings

- The coin in its mouth signifies increased income.

- The baby tortoise on its back symbolizes wonderful descendants' luck, which usually means many sons.

You can use this symbol as a paperweight. Place it on your desk either in the north or east sector but not if this is directly in front of you. Try to have it by the side of you. You can also place this symbol behind where you sit to signify that you have the support of both the dragon and the tortoise.

Do not put this symbol directly in front of you as if you were confronting it. In feng shui, when you confront a powerful symbol, you are asking for trouble.

A pot of gold or a wealth chest under the rainbow

Symbols of wealth and money in feng shui need not always come from the Chinese tradition. When you understand the origins of feng shui symbolism, and the

Pot of Gold

fundamentals upon which its correct placements are based, you will find that if wealth luck is based on actual physical manifestations of wealth, everything that connotes money and a fortune in gold can be used to feign the positive energies associated with wealth luck. I have discovered for example that many of the old masters describe the contents of *wealth vases* and *wealth chests* in almost the same way that Western fairy tales describe them. Like the pot of gold under the rainbow or the pirate's chest of treasures, these remind me of the pile of gold ingots and coins upon which various creatures of good fortune sit.

Thus if you want to stimulate symbolic feng shui in your home, and you don't want it looking too much like a Chinese curio shop, you can do what I do. You can energize your living rooms with beautiful crystals fashioned into wealth chests filled with *faux* or fake precious jewels. I use crystal bowls and fill them with coloured glass that look like jewels and then place them near windows to catch the *rainbows* made by the sun shining on my hanging cut crystal balls. They look very beautiful and also bring in plenty of yang energy. Crystals are a great medium for feng shui symbolism because crystals represent earth energy.

Feng shui is all about harnessing the luck from the earth, and it is only from the earth that gold or precious metal is found. Remember that in the productive cycle of the

Always cleanse your personal crystal by soaking it in a sea-salt solution for 7 days and 7 nights.

Wu Xing or five elements, earth produces metal, and the Chinese character for metal is gold! Thus when you energize for the earth element with crystals, you are energizing for gold, the symbol of wealth. If you wish, you can display a natural quartz crystal. Place this kind of crystal energizer in the NW or West to activate the gold energy of these two sectors. Select crystals according to your own taste.

Display the tribute horse to signify victory

The Chinese always associate the *tribute horse* with gifts given to emperors and other powerful court officials. From the times of the Sung emperors through to the imperial rulers of the Qing dynasty, the tribute horse has always been associated with gifts brought by the vanquished to the victors. Thus the tribute horse symbolizes the spoils of battle. If you are involved in a very competitive situation, placing a painting with the tribute horse as the subject is one of the best ways of using symbolic feng shui to bring you victory luck. This is because the horse signifies triumph over your competitors. If you cannot find such a painting, look for something that shows a horse (preferably white) that is laden with precious things and that is being led (not ridden) by an official. This symbolizes upward mobility and promotion. It is very auspicious indeed, especially if the horse is white.

The horse is very favourably regarded as one of the precious animals that emits a great deal of yang energy. The horse is also one of the *precious* animals included in the mandala offering to Buddha. It is emblematic of nobility, class and a comfortable lifestyle. It stands for speed and perseverance. The horse should always be placed **South** in your house, and this means the South wall or corner of any of the rooms as well. It is best placed in the living and family areas and never in the bedrooms.

Do not display a horse that is rearing up and worse yet, do not place such a rearing horse directly behind you or directly

Place the tribute horse in the South to symbolise enhancing your authority luck

confronting you. You will suffer accidents and physical problems related to your limbs if you do that. Instead, let the horse be placed in a non-threatening posture. Some wonderful replicas of auspicious horses are the famous Ming horse sculptures that are ideal for the South part of your living room.

Elephants bring Descendant Luck

A pair of precious elephants for success and descendants luck

The word for elephant in Chinese sounds like *hsiang*, which can also mean Prime Minister. The elephant is thus the symbol of strength, prudence, energy and sound judgment - all the qualities of a good and moral leader. It is also one of the four animals that represent power (the other three being the tiger, the lion and the leopard). The elephant is also regarded as one of the seven treasures of Buddhism and features strongly as one of the precious animals that is significantly included in the Mandala offering made to Buddhist deities at pujas. In Thailand, the white elephant is regarded as a holy animal, and in many Oriental cultures, Deities and Gods are often depicted riding atop an elephant. In Chinese culture, pictures of children seated on elephants is said to represent good fortune.

The feng shui significance of the elephant is that it brings plenty of good fortune associated with the rise of the patriarch to power and prominence. This is because the elephant is believed to be the **bearer of the wish granting jewel** so that its symbolic presence in the home signifies the luck of having all one's aspirations granted. The ideal way of displaying the elephant in the home is to buy a pair of ceramic elephants and place them either inside or outside of the house, and on either side of the main entrance door. I prefer them inside my house to symbolize the arrival of good luck. Mine are a pair of those wonderful and inexpensive ceramic elephants imported from Vietnam.

The elephant is also said to be an excellent symbol for granting descendants luck to households. It is believed that childless women who have the image of the elephant in the bedroom will enhance their chances of getting a male child.

In the outskirts of Beijing near the Ming tombs, there are gigantic stone elephants standing and kneeling along the avenue leading to the tombs. Women wanting male children often rub the stern of these elephants to invoke the energy of the male child.

Discover the gem spouting mongoose and the *power of the pi yao*

The Chinese preoccupation with harnessing prosperity luck and overcoming bad luck is so pronounced that there are many animals which symbolize getting wealth and overcoming bad luck. Some of these animals are easy to identify, but others can a bit tricky. I would like to introduce you to two symbols which you can place on your desk as wealth energizers, as well as to overcome bad feng shui.

Gem Spouting Moongoose

The mongoose resembles the domestic rat. Above, he is shown sitting on a bed of gold ingots and coins. The mongoose is said to spout precious gems and jewels from its mouth. He is featured as the principal wealth creator carried by all three of the Tibetan Buddhas of Wealth, the White Jambhala, the Yellow Jambhala and the Black Jambhala. Followers of Tibetan Buddhism often display this Buddha of Wealth sitting under a fountain of water, since this is believed to please him and will cause the mongoose to spout forth plenty of valuable gemstones and jewels.

The Pi Yao (also known as the Pik Chen) are earth and sea variations of a particularly

The Pi Yao also regarded as the Dragon Dog, is capable of appeasing the Grand Duke who is the Deity of the year.

White Jambhala with the moongoose

powerful and auspicious creature of good fortune. He is said to have the power of assisting anyone suffering from bad feng shui that is due to having offended the Grand Duke Jupiter (Tai Sui). Those enduring a period of bad luck soon after moving into a new home or soon after undertaking renovations should display the image of the Pi Yao or Pik Chen in the home.

The Red Bat is a yang symbol of good fortune

The red bat has been an auspicious emblem of prosperity, happiness and longevity for a very long time. The origin of this positive connotation of what could well have been an obnoxious creature comes from the sound of its name. In Chinese it is known as

the *pian fu,* and the word *fu* also sounds like happiness and good fortune. As such, the bat is a very popular symbol that is frequently used for decorative purposes. When utilized for feng shui reasons, the bat is usually painted in a cinnabar red. This is because red is also the colour of joy. Usually, red bats are drawn in a cluster of five, and this is the pictorial representation of the five blessings from heaven - old age or longevity; wealth; health, love of virtue and a natural death. **Five red bats** also represent the yang symbol of prosperity. These are usually drawn onto ceramics and paintings. One of the more auspicious representations is of five bats emerging from a jar or vase. This means not only happiness and good fortune but also a peaceful life with few problems.

The Chinese believe that if a family of bats takes up residence in your home, it is an exceptionally good omen. It signifies the coming of a time of prosperity and success for the household. Thus bats should never be chased away. Last year, a family of bats took up residence in the home of a friend of mine. I urged him to make the bats welcome. Since then his business has prospered by leaps and bounds. According to a Chinese legend, there are silver coloured bats that live for a thousand years. They live deep inside caverns in the high mountains feeding on stalactites. If you can find them and eat them, you will live to a very ripe old age!

Bats are especially auspicious when displayed with other symbols

In the days of the Manchu emperors, bats were second in popularity only to the imperial dragon. Of all the auspicious symbols sewn onto the imperial robes, perhaps the most frequently encountered symbol was that of the red bat. It was usually interspersed with clouds and water motifs as shown on the Dragon robe here.

> Five bats signify the five blessings of longevity, wealth, health, a life of virtue and a natural death.

5 Bats with swastika and the longevity symbol shown here combine the imagery of three symbols. These symbols together signify a long life filled with great joy and riches. Ideally the bats are painted red. This symbol can be embroidered onto clothes, painted on vases and urns or incorporated into logos and paintings. Place them prominently in the living or dining room to enjoy continuous good fortune.

Enhancing & protecting the family rice urn

If your staple food is rice, always take care of the family rice urn. It does not matter how you keep your rice, and in what sort of container, but here are some useful ways you can ensure that your symbolic rice bowl is always protected, thereby ensuring that your family's fortunes never take a turn for the worse.

- Always keep the rice urn closed. Apart from keeping rats and cockroaches out, this also signifies that your family wealth is protected.

- Do not use a plastic bin to keep your rice. This is inauspicious. Instead, use something that is made of ceramic or clay. The earth energy is very sound and solid. Some people like to keep their rice in wooden urns and this too is good.

- Do not allow water to seep or drip into the rice urn. This makes the rice go bad and is not a good sign.

- Place a red packet with real money inside your rice urn, at the very bottom. Or trace these symbols of gold ornaments (shown below) on red paper and put them in your urn. Always top up with a fresh red packet at the start of every lunar new year - this symbolizes that your family fortunes can only increase and never decrease.

- Never allow your rice urn to get empty. It is a good idea to replenish as soon as the urn is half full. There is nothing as inauspicious as a rice urn that is allowed to get empty. Remember, in feng shui, containers should never be left empty, so when you give a gift of a pretty container to someone, always fill the container with something. Any bad luck will boomerang on you.

- Keep the rice urn hidden away inside a larder, storeroom or cupboard. This will ensure you do not lose your wealth or get robbed.

- There are no hard and fast rules regarding the shape of the rice urn, but a deeper urn is better than a shallow one. When the urn is deep, it signifies that you have deep pockets with lots of money. If the rice urn is shallow, it suggests that you could run short of money.

- Do not allow anyone to empty the family rice urn, or the rice cooker, as this is considered the worst kind of bad feng shui! In fact, the upsetting of a container of rice on the table or elsewhere is considered so unlucky that in the old days, servants careless enough to do this were thrown out of the home immediately. Today, the rice cooker is where most families cook and serve their rice. Do not ever let this be upset or overturned. There is no worse omen of bad luck than this. So make certain your rice urn and cooker sit solidly on firm surfaces.

Golden chopsticks,
the money tree & the wish fulfilling cow

One of the best gifts to give someone is a pair of **golden chopsticks**, although this is one of the lesser known good fortune symbols. I was so thrilled at the start of this year when I was presented with two pairs of chopsticks

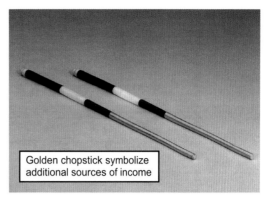

Golden chopstick symbolize additional sources of income

with matching horse shoe chopstick holders. One pair was *gold* and the other pair was *silver*. I consider this an extremely auspicious gift and am currently displaying them quite ostentatiously in my dining room for good luck. Chopsticks symbolize additional sources of income.

There are a couple of taboos when it comes to chopsticks, and it is useful to familiarize yourself with them:

- Never leave two chopsticks standing on a bowl of rice. This is the sign of death and is regarded with tremendous disfavour, especially during the lunar New Year.

- Never lend chopsticks to anyone. If someone wishes to borrow your chopsticks, offer to *symbolically sell them for a penny*. Giving away your chopsticks, even if it is only on loan, is like giving away your livelihood.

a holy animal. For good luck, display the cow sitting on a bed of coins and ingots anywhere on your desk.

Golden ingots can be used to fill wealth ships, wealth vases and urns

Gold Ingots

Gold Ingots attract an abundance of wealth luck and continuous good fortune into the home. The display of gold ingots is always auspicious because it signifies wealth and material assets, representing savings and worth. Place as many of these gold ingots as you wish inside wealth vases, wealth bowls and sailing ships in your home and office.

Lapis Lazuli Globe

The globe is a potent representation of the earth element. When made of a semiprecious stone such as lapis lazuli, it is an excellent energizer for the luck of knowledge and self-development. Place it in the Northeast corner of your home and twirl it daily to create the movement that stirs up auspicious chi. I have always kept such a globe to activate the business corner of my house and to activate auspicious Chi so my books would sell all around the world!

The Money Tree

There seems to be several variations of the money tree. In Chinese texts on feng shui, reference is often made to the legendary money tree on which is said to hang strings of gold coins and ingots. Like the tree, which is said to bear the fruit of immortality, the money tree is as much mythical as it is symbolic. A popular variation is the wish fulfilling gem tree that is made of precious stones and displayed for good fortune.

The Wish Fulfilling Cow

Like the elephant in Thailand, the cow holds a special place in the hearts of the people of India. In feng shui, reference is made to the wish-fulfilling cow, which is said to be emblematic of good descendants' luck. In Buddhism and Hinduism, the cow is regarded as

Wish-fulfilling Cow

Chapter Two:
Symbols of Longevity

The Chinese believe that there is no good luck without long life. Good feng shui creates longevity for the family patriarch and matriarch. Enhance the longevity and life span of all members of your household by displaying symbols of longevity in the home and magnify their effect by placing them in the best feng shui orientation. Longevity does not mean only a healthy life, but also one that is protected from fatal and life threatening accidents and mishaps.

To the Chinese, longevity is one of three significant aspirations. Every prayer and every salutation includes the wish for long life!

To enjoy good health and a smooth ride through life, consider displaying the beautiful **Crane**, the evergreen **Pine Tree**, and the succulent fruit of longevity, the **Peach.** Invite in **Sau** - the **Deity of Longevity** and place him high in a place of honour. Take note of his constant companion, the agile and auspicious **Deer**. Grow a patch of long lasting **bamboo**, or create a **tortoise pond** to capture the essence of this celestial creature's many auspicious qualities.

Display a **jade cicada** to signify the good life in the after life. These and many more are the symbols that fulfill this significant aspiration. Use them to complement and enhance your feng shui practice.

Remember that everything you do to enhance longevity also implies creating good health luck for the family and for all the residents in the house. Supplement this by being aware of the period or time stars of flying star feng shui which can bring illness and accidents. Thus in addition to longevity energizers and enhancers, also study the table and texts in Chapter 10 to personalize the feng shui of residents according to the application of symbols to counteract bad flying stars.

Invite the God of Longevity SAU into your house

Sau, the God of Longevity is probably one of the most popular Deities found in many Chinese homes. He is one of the three star Gods that are collectively known as **Fuk Luk Sau**.

The God of Longevity is usually depicted in paintings, drawn onto porcelain and ceramics, and is also carved in wood, ivory and stone. He is popular because he symbolizes good health and a smooth and long life. He is usually dressed in a yellow robe and carries a staff with the magical gourd tied to the top.

The gourd itself is an auspicious symbol which, when carried by the God of Longevity, is said to be filled with the nectar of Immortality. Sau often carries the peach, the fruit of immortality, and sometimes a crane and a deer also accompany him. In the picture here, Sau is shown standing holding a staff with a bottle gourd of nectar in one hand, and the peach, the fruit of immortality, in the other. At other times, Sau is drawn with the pine tree, surrounded by longevity mushrooms known as *ling chi*. This is often referred to as the plant of long life.

Place **Sau** in a high place in full view of the entrance into the room where he is located. Place him with a solid wall behind. It is considered bad luck to have a window, toilet or kitchen directly behind, or directly

Sau, the God of Longevity

in front of him. The best place for Sau is on a table placed in the corner that is diagonal to the door.

The God of Longevity is not a Buddhist deity. He is not worshipped in the same way that Buddha is worshipped. Do not place Sau on your altar, since doing so does not make him more auspicious in any way. There is no necessity to treat Sau as a God in the western sense. But it is also not lucky to place him on a table that is too low. When he is placed too low, there is an implied lack of respect for what he stands for. The coffee table is not a suitable place for him. The rule of thumb is that all symbolic deities placed in the home should ideally be at eye level with the residents of the household.

The beautiful Crane is endowed with many mythical attributes

The Crane has a reputation of being the patriarch of all feathered creatures of the earth. Next to the phoenix, he is the most favoured of all the bird symbols of good fortune. He is the Bird of Immortality and is strongly

Place the longevity crane on the West side of your garden to benefit the old folk in your home.

identified with the attributes of long life, happiness and smoothness of flight. His symbolic presence in the home or garden is believed to bring harmony and happiness to the home. It was these attributes that prompted me to display flower pots with crane and pine tree designs, and to search for a marble crane sculpture to place in the South sector of my garden. I regard my cranes with great fondness and am convinced they bring me many opportunities as well as a smooth and happy life.

There are four types of cranes in Chinese mythology, black, white, yellow and blue cranes. Of the four, the black crane is reputed to live the longest. He is said to live for 600 years.

The use of cranes as symbols of good fortune, and particularly as symbols of longevity, go back to the time of the legendary emperor Fu Hsi. Stories of the adventures of the Eight Immortals are peppered with references to the white crane. Drawn onto Chinese art and craft objects, the crane is shown in many different poses, each of which convey subtle shades of meanings of good fortune.

- Shown flying and soaring to heaven, the crane symbolizes a good afterlife, since the crane is often viewed as the conveyor of souls to heaven. For this reason, some consider it auspicious to place a crane with outspread wings and uplifted foot in the center of a coffin during the funeral procession. This was believed to guide the soul safely to heaven.

- Shown amongst clouds, the crane symbolizes longevity, wisdom and a life close to the emperor. Thus it signifies reaching a high position of power.

- Shown frolicking amongst pine trees, it denotes staying power, resilience and a life filled with honours and wealth.

Shown as a pair, cranes signify the long life of the family patriarch and matriarch

One of the best anniversary gifts to present to one's parents is artwork that shows a pair of white cranes nestled between branches of the pine tree. This denotes continuation of the family unit intact with both patriarch and matriarch. The real meaning however goes deeper. It also signifies the continuation of all the best qualities of the chien and kun trigrams as well as the protection of family harmony and wellbeing. White cranes (those with the tuft of red on the head) are believed to bring harmony into households, ensuring all relationships within the family are harmonious.

Cranes also signify wisdom, the kind that solves all problems and dissolves all obstacles that stand in the way of the family's upward progression. The flying crane signifies attainment of great heights with honour, while a single crane gazing upwards at the sun or moon signifies aspiring to the ultimate wisdom. The white crane is therefore a very desirable symbol to display in the home.

The best corner of the home for the crane is the South. This brings opportunities. Placed in the West, the crane brings good luck for the children, while placed in the Northwest it favours the family patriarch. Placed in the East, the Crane benefits the sons of the family and especially the eldest son. Screens that have cranes drawn on them make excellent feng shui cures when there are three or more doors in a straight line within the home. Or when you simply wish to block out unlucky sights.

The sectors that do not benefit from the crane's presence is the kitchen, bathrooms and toilets. It is acceptable to display cranes in bedrooms, dining rooms and family rooms.

The Pine tree is unswerving, firm and resolute - the ultimate symbol of inner strength

The pine tree is probably the strongest symbol of inner strength and permanence. In the cold winter months, the pine does not lose its needles, thereby manifesting its steadfastness, strength and fortitude. The pine is a favourite symbol of longevity and probably the most frequently painted tree. Almost all landscape paintings show the pine with rocks and narcissus which indicate a life of long-lasting personal achievements; or with the bamboo and the plum tree. Together, these represent the *three friends in winter*. Painted together, they signify friendship in adversity, through thick and thin.

The pine tree is also a popular subject of poetry. In the works of Confucius, there are many references to the pine, most of the time used as a metaphor or allegory to illustrate its attributes of steadfastness and survival under difficult conditions. Old pine trees are regarded with the greatest respect, so if you have grown pines in your garden, do treat them with respect. A pair of healthy pine trees in the garden is also a *symbol of married bliss*.

Shown to the left here is a typical landscape painting complete with mountain and water - the two most important ingredients of good landscape feng shui. In the foreground is the pine tree, its lush growth of needles indicating it is the time of summer.

This painting expresses the wish for a long life of plenty and abundance. The water flowing inwards, towards you in a most excellent orientation.

Peach Tree for long life

Peaches for immortality and long life and as a symbol of marriage opportunity

No other tree or fruit has greater depth of symbolic meaning than the peach tree. Every part of this plant is believed to possess some valuable attribute. Peach wood is said to be wonderful protection against naughty spirits and demons. In the old days, weapons like bows and arrows would be made of peach wood. Taoist priests also used peach wood to make their seals with

which to signet their amulets and talismans with protective luck.

At the same time, peach blooms and petals were believed to possess the power to cast romantic spells over men! Taoist magic love spells are said to require the use of the peach blossom to be effective. Sad to say I do not have the formula for making these love potions!

It is however the peach fruit that is said to be most valuable. Legend has it that the peach plant of immortality stood somewhere in the holy *Kun Lun* mountains of China, in the fabled gardens of the Goddess of the West, **Hsi Wang Mu.** This miraculous tree was said to bear the peach fruit of immortality only once every three thousand years, and once when it did, the Goddess invited the Eight Immortals to her garden for a feast. This was how they attained the status of immortality. Alas, just as the party got underway, along came the Monkey God (together with a retinue of others) who harvested all the peaches and himself attained immortality! Thus placing the image of the Monkey God stealing the peaches of immortality in your home is said to endow the home with a great deal of longevity energies. I have just such a wood sculpture in my home. I bought this many years ago in Fukien province in China and was told this beautiful legend that lay behind the symbolic meaning of the sculpture.

The peach is also the symbol of Springtime, for it is during this time that the peach tree blooms in China. Spring is said to be the best time for couples to get married, and the peach is also a symbol of marriage. Placing a picture of peaches in one's room is believed to create the *chi of marriage*, thereby enhancing marriage opportunities for single men and women of the family. Get a jadeite peach plant and display in the Southwest to bring you marriage happiness.

The Bamboo is durable and resilient signifying longevity and fortitude

The bamboo has long been regarded as a symbol of longevity, due primarily to its durability. The plant stays evergreen through the four seasons and in all conditions of growth. It even flourishes in the winter months thereby earning for itself the attributes of resilience and fortitude. In China, the bamboo plant grows throughout the country, as far north as Beijing. There are some ten species of bamboo and within each species, there are many different varieties. All varieties of the bamboo can

Bamboo brings resilience and longevity

be displayed to actualize the symbolism of longevity.

There are different legends associated with different varieties of bamboo. The *spotted bamboo* signifies undying love and fidelity as they are said to be the tears of the emperor's consorts. The *spiny bamboo* has more leaves than stems and this variety signifies the luck of old age associated with good family luck. The Patriarch will have the good fortune to share the successes of the descendants. The *solid stemmed bamboo* signifies a life that is free of illness and disease. Good health is associated with these sturdy versions of the bamboo plant.

In the old days, the growing of bamboo groves epitomized the symbolic presence of longevity chi. Those wanting to manifest the bamboo plant can do so by placing potted bamboo plants near the front part of the home, or better yet, along the East side of the garden. This is the sector of the wood element and is ideal for placing the auspicious bamboo.

It is a good idea to hang classical paintings of the *leafy bamboo* in the study or office to ensure longevity of good fortune associated with work and career. Select paintings that show groups of dangling bamboo leaves in numbers that are auspicious. In this connection, groups of 6, 8 and 9 leaves (or multiples thereof) are deemed to be auspicious while groups of five, seven, two and three leaves are deemed to be less auspicious. The best combinations are bamboo leaves in groups of 6 and 8.

Bamboo calligraphy signifies good luck associated with resilience in adversity

The bamboo is also a symbol of endurance and protection. In winter, many homes in China would have groves of bamboo plants that act as shields against the cold north winds. Thus, bamboo grown in the North part of the garden symbolizes protection. If your home suffers from cold winds and require protection during the winter months, plant a curtain of bamboo where it most effectively shelters you irrespective of the direction. The bamboo is also a very hardy plant. Biologically, it is regarded as a kind of grass and yet it can grow taller than many trees. Bamboo thrive on almost any kind of soil, and it is continuously green despite weather conditions. It endures through the coldest of winters and the hottest of summers. When the wind blows, it bends

with the flow, sometimes bending as low as the ground itself. This signifies the way difficulties should be faced. The bamboo bends, adapts, goes with the flow, but it never changes itself. And after the storm, it always survives.

The bamboo is considered the perfect metaphor for humanity and life. As such, it is a popular subject for artists and calligraphers, who take joy in perfecting the different strokes that make up both the stalks and the leaves of the bamboo.

Calligraphy is the art of writing beautifully and this represents perfect balance between motion and pressure. The Chinese brush is amazingly flexible and good calligraphy signifies perfect balance created by the brush.

Good calligraphy is also the end result of exceedingly good chi energy; thus it suggests good feng shui especially when the characters being written represent auspicious words. When the subject is bamboo, the combination of the subject and calligraphy signifies good luck associated with a long and happy life that survives through bad times and adversity. Bamboo with calligraphy is best displayed in the study or library.

The Deer has many good meanings

The deer symbolizes longevity and a whole lot more

By any name, or found anywhere, the deer is a very popular symbol associated with speed, endurance and long life. In the Yangtze valley, the deer resembles the antelope and in the Southwestern mountains of China in the mountains bordering on Tibet, he looks like the yak.

Phonetically, the deer in Chinese sounds like the word *lu*, which also means good income and prosperity. As such, the deer also signifies wealth. Together with its other meaning, the deer means a long life filled with wealth and prosperity. It is therefore extremely auspicious to have the image of the deer in the office of businessmen and women. Displayed in the work place, the deer symbolizes the wish for the company to prosper and grow. Displayed at home, it means the family

living there will enjoy a long life of ease and growing prosperity.

There are many folk legends associated with the deer in central and North Asia, but in Chinese mythology, he is almost always shown accompanying Sau, the God of Longevity.

Many Chinese artists also like to depict the deer next to a high court official, since this represents the wish that recipient will achieve fame, riches and a long career. This makes it an excellent gift for someone who wishes to advance in his or her career, or for someone who has just graduated and is embarking on a working career.

Since the deer is generally regarded as light footed, speedy and endowed with great endurance, these are the attributes being wished for when its image is displayed. Those wishing to have the deer in the house, either get a painting of Sau with the deer or search for the deer standing on a bed of coins and gold ingots that symbolize wealth.

A jade cicada is an emblem of Immortality and amulet against politics

To the Chinese, the cicada is a most powerful emblem of Immortality, and in the old days, rich families would often bury their dead with a piece of jade carved in the form of a cicada in the corpse's mouth. It was believed that this would immortalize the ancestor, giving him or her a good life after death.

For the living, the cicada was regarded as a symbol of long life, happiness and eternal youth. This was probably due to the fact that the cicada is the longest living insect. Some say it lives for as long as eighteen years!

The origin of this symbolism can also be attributed to the legend of the cicada being in reality an ancient Queen who did many good deeds during her reign. On her death, she was believed to have been reborn a cicada. As a cicada she never grew old physically, and she lived longer than all other insects. The cicada since then became a symbol of youthfulness of appearance.

The cicada is also believed to be a symbol of protection. It is said that when you wear an image of the cicada on your body, you will be warned and protected from danger, from the approach of unfaithful friends and from enemies. Court officials often hid a jade cicada in their robes to protect them against falling victim to Court intrigues and politics. In this regard, it can be looked upon as an amulet of some kind. Corporate players in the modern business environment requiring protection against jealous colleagues or scheming bosses might find it useful to search for a jade cicada to wear as a pendant amulet around their neck.

These can be found in China Arts and Crafts shops in Hong Kong, or the jade boutiques of Taiwan, Singapore and China. Failing this, look for a cicada paperweight and place it on your desk in the office. Naturally, if you cannot afford it in jade, look for it made of a material that simulates and looks like the translucent jade.

Another attribute of the cicada is its singing ability. The male cicada sings throughout the summer to attract the female. This is very favorably regarded as a good fortune omen.

The tortoise is the best symbol of longevity to have around the house

I have found that nothing beats the tortoise for bringing good feng shui into the home. It is a symbol of multi-dimensional meaning and is the only one of the celestial creatures that actually exists and is easy to find. The tortoise is not merely a symbol of longevity, although having his real presence in the home is said to ensure that family patriarchs live to well beyond 80 years of age! The tortoise is also a symbol of protection, of support and of wealth and prosperity.

In feng shui, the tortoise signifies the protective hills of the North as well as the back support that ensures the house stays firm and strong. The tortoise was also the bearer of the magical Lo Shu square of numbers, which it was said to have carried on its back and brought to the attention of Fu Hsi. This was the first legendary emperor of China to whom is attributed the authorship of the Book of Changes or I Ching upon which all feng shui theory is based. There are many more legends that describe the mystical and enigmatic symbolism of the tortoise.

The tortoise is the only celestial creature still in existence. It is very beneficial to have tortoises in the home.

The tortoise is said to conceal within its body and within the design motifs on its shell all the secrets of heaven and earth. I myself started writing books about feng shui soon after I picked up the shell of a dead turtle washed up on shore on a seaside vacation trip to Pangkor Island with my family. That was in 1992. At that time, I failed to note the significance of that fateful omen, and although I brought the shell back home, I discarded it soon afterwards. I only realized the symbolism of that sign while one day meditating by my pond where my pet terrapins lived. (Terrapins are domestic tortoises and turtles are the marine relations of the freshwater tortoise).

My story of course pales into inconsequence next to the many legends of the tortoise. A magical tortoise was said to have helped the Emperor to tame the raging Yellow River (the *Hwang Ho*). It is also believed that when **Pan Ku** created the world, he used tortoises as pillars to hold up the Universe. The tortoise's humped back was the sky, its belly was the earth and its legendary longevity made it indestructible.

Even better would be a display of the Dragon Tortoise on a bed of coins

If you examine a live tortoise carefully, you will see that it has the head of a snake and a very long neck, which many suggest resembles the dragon!

Thus, embodied in this creature, which still walks the face of the earth is the *spirit of the dragon*. Feng shui practitioners often display the dragon tortoise as a symbol of great good fortune inside their homes. This

Dragon Tortoise

creature is frequently fashioned sitting on a bed of coins and gold ingots. In its mouth is a single coin of a prosperous reign period such as the reign period of the Emperor Kangsu or the Emperor Chien Lung. Such a symbol embodies both the bravery of the dragon and the shielding qualities of the tortoise. Business people who place this image behind them at the office will find the business risks they take will be bolder, yet less risky. The bed of coins indicates the successful accumulation of wealth and prosperity. Images such as the one shown here are easy to find in Chinese curio shops and supermarkets in Chinatown. They should not be expensive and are usually made of plaster painted with gold paint, or made of brass and can be quite heavy. Displaying *one* is sufficient. There is no need to overdo the imagery by having too many of this creature.

While I like the image here, and therefore have it in my office at home, I also like keeping real live terrapins. My terrapins live in the North sector of my home. This sector is where my flying star numbers are the most excellent. I have the 6 as my mountain star and the 8 as my water star. As such, instead of one, I keep 6 terrapins in the water. To energize the water element, I also created a miniature waterfall falling into a small pond. I make very sure the water is falling towards the home, and not flowing away, since this would symbolize money flowing out. It is in the pond that I keep my terrapins. Those unfamiliar with flying star feng shui can keep a single terrapin in the North. You do not need to build an elaborate water feature. A small bowl or basin half filled

with water should do nicely. Allow some rocks for the terrapin to sun himself on warm sunny days. This also encourages the accumulation of yang energy in the North sector. The result of this water feature with terrapins benefits your career and brings wonderful opportunities for advancement at work.

The gourd signifies an abundance of blessings

The bottle gourd, known also as the *Wu Lou*, is both a Taoist and Buddhist symbol of good fortune. It is a powerful *tool of Taoist magic* and also considered a *receptacle of the holy nectar* of many Buddhist Deities. It is featured in many old paintings of both traditions. Thus the God of Longevity carries a staff at the end of which is a bottle gourd said to contain the elixir of Immortality. The immensely popular Buddhist

Wu Lou brings good health luck

Bodhisattva, Kuan Yin (or the Goddess of Mercy) carries a small vial filled with her blessing nectar. This vial is often shaped like the bottle gourd. The gourd is also the symbol carried by one of the Eight Immortals **Lee Tie Guai**. From the gourd is emitted a spiral of incense, which represents his special ability of separating his physical body from his soul consciousness. This is supposedly a manifestation of the spiritual mysticism that surrounds this symbol, and indeed the gourd is a very popular and prominent accessory of Deities of the Taoist and Buddhist pantheon.

This may be due to the fact that the shape of the gourd is a representation of heaven and earth united in miniature, and this, it is believed, accounts for its shape. This is also the shape most favoured for making wealth vases. The top half is heaven and the bottom half is earth. Displaying a dried gourd in and around the home is a good omen. It suggests that the home receives much blessings and is visited by these holy beings. It is probably for this reason also that many temples are decorated with many such bottle gourds.

The gourd design shown above suggests ten thousand years of springtime. When the gourd is decorated with many children, it means ten thousand generations of male descendants, and when drawn with peaches and other longevity symbols, it means ten thousand generations of long living patriarchs. In other words, the gourd magnifies and multiplies all good fortune meanings indicated by other symbols of good fortune. Merely wearing a small miniature of the gourd fashioned in gold around the neck is said to ward off pernicious influences and accidents, since it is such a powerful longevity symbol.

The Eight Immortals or Paht Hseen are Taoist images of Immortality

The Eight Immortals are superior beings of Taoist legend. Comprising six men and two women, these beings are said to have lived at various times. They each attained immortality under different circumstances, but legend says they have each tasted the nectar and peach of Immortality! The Eight Immortals are widely regarded as symbols of longevity and good fortune. They are frequently depicted in Chinese porcelain - vases and urns - to symbolize their good fortune attributes. They are also drawn onto plates, usually as a group of eight crossing the waters or singly, wielding their respective symbols. They are also depicted in ivory, wood and bronze. Students of the Chinese traditions sometimes compare them to the Buddhist Eighteen Arhats - enlightened beings said to have brought Buddhism to China and each also holding a personal symbol.

The Eight Beings (*Hseen*) and the 18 Arhats (*Loharn*) are said to possess supernatural powers and are capable of performing magic. Their symbolic presence in homes, on paintings or as statues in any medium are believed to bestow good health, happiness and general good fortune on families. It is for this reason that they are such popular subjects of artists and craftsmen. Each of the Eight Immortals represents some special life circumstance and each holds a symbol that expresses a significant ability or power. If you display them singly in your home, it is useful to understand what they each signify.

The Eight Immortals bestow happiness, good health and excellent fortune.

The chief of the 8 Immortals is **Han Zhong Li,** who is generally shown as fat, with a bare belly and holding a fan which he uses to revive sick people. He is said to symbolize good health and to possess curative powers. Displayed in the home, he is said to cause residents to enjoy good health and live a healthy long life.

The second Immortal is **Zhang Guo Lao,** who carries a musical instrument shaped like a bamboo tube. He is said to possess the wisdom of the ages and has the ability to make himself invisible. This Immortal is regarded as a sage, whose image bestows wisdom on the family patriarch.

The Immortals signify wealth & poverty, age & youth, male & female, nobility & commoner

The third Immortal is **Lee Dong Bin,** a scholar recluse regarded as the patron saint of the sick. He is said to have learnt much of his magic craft from the chief of the Immortals. On his back is a sword, which he uses to overcome evil spirits and slice through

sufferings caused by bad energies. In his right hand is a fly whisk, which he uses to cure illnesses. Displayed in the home, this Immortal protects against illness caused by evil spirits and bad chi.

The fourth Immortal is **Chao Guo Jiu,** reputed to have been related to an Empress of the Sung Dynasty. He signifies nobility and is depicted dressed in official robes. His symbol is a pair of castanets, which he holds high up in his left hand. These symbolize his noble birth. Tsao is said to bestow recognition and attract high office for the family patriarch. Politicians and those wishing for a life of power should invite his image into the home.

The fifth Immortal is **Lee Tie Guai,** who looks like a beggar, but is reputed to be the Master of Supernatural Ability.

The sixth Immortal is **Han Xiang Zi,** who makes sweet sounds with his flute. This attracts good fortune *chi* around him, so all animals, insects and plants thrive profusely in his presence. Han's special ability is to make plants bloom instantly. He keeps a profusion of plants in the sack he carries on his back.

The seventh Immortal is **Lan Chai He.** He carries a flower basket and is said to epitomize the spirit of femininity.

The eighth Immortal is another woman, a fairy called **He Xian Gu.** Her emblem is the holy lotus and the fly whisk. Her presence in the home benefits the matriarch.

Place the 8 Immortals according to the Pa Kua directions to generate great good fortune

Symbolic feng shui borrows much from the Taoist legends, and the Eight Immortals symbolize the pinnacle of life aspirations. Place images of the Immortals in your home either collectively in a painting or individually according to the Eight directions. Each of the Immortals is said to signify one of the directions and should thus be placed accordingly to energize that direction. Follow the representations indicated in the table below.

No	Name of Immortal	Direction	Element	Symbol	Special Benefit
1	Han Zhong Li	East	Wood	Fan & Peach	Longevity and ceaseless energy
2	Zhang Guo Lao	North	Water	Bamboo flute	Childless couples: Put in bedrooms to conceive children
3	Lee Dong Bin	West	Metal	Sword & fly whisk	Cures illness, good scholar luck
4	Chao Guo Jiu	Northeast	Earth	Castanets	Bestows luck to those who want power
5	Lee Tie Guai	South	Fire	Bottle gourd	Bestows wisdom. Most powerful of the 8
6	Han Xiang Zi	Southeast	Wood	Flute	Healing energies
7	Lan Chai He	Northwest	Metal	Flower basket	Health & Education
8	He Xian Gu	Southwest	Earth	Lotus	Family & marriage luck

Display the herb of immortality to activate career success in public life

It is not a widely known fact that the herb of immortality, also referred to as **ling zhi**, bestows not merely the promise of immortal life, but also rapid growth, and brings with it the luck of success in careers

ling zhi plant

that require public interface. Basically, it is excellent for those engaged in politics and entertainment. In fact, the herb is frequently referred to in Chinese classical literature, and paintings of the deer, the crane and other symbols of longevity always include a drawing of this grass-like plant.

In appearance, the herb resembles grass. Legend describes it as growing on the mountain face located on a Holy Island in the secret oceans. It looks like water-grass, being long, oval and pointed. When boiled and drunk with water, the herb of immortality is said to make you live to a ripe old age. Some texts describe it as one kind of mushroom complete with stalk and cap. It would be fantasy to imagine we could ever get access to such a herb, but the imagery of such grass when drawn onto

paintings or when carved onto furniture is said to bring long life and auspicious upward mobility luck. It is believed that when the image of this herb is carved onto family altars, residents will enjoy long and healthy lives. In the same way, if altars are carved with prosperity symbols such as the bat or the fish, the family enjoys great wealth.

Other elixirs of immortality are various mystical compounds which Taoist alchemists have made legendary with their claims of immortality and magic. Thus, **red cinnabar** is said to possess magical attributes. Auspicious characters written in cinnabar offer *transcendental* feng shui enhancement, while protective words written in this red powder are said to create magical amulets for personal protection. Cinnabar is said to bestow long life, and water from a well lined with cinnabar is said to be excellent for extending life.

The Chinese also believe that the **ginseng root** has life extension attributes as well. As a result of this, there are certain varieties of ginseng root that are sold for incredible sums of money! A wild rumour has it that Chinese leaders have access to this fabulously magical ginseng potion, thereby accounting for the long lives of most of the Chinese leadership. Finally, the other most fabled elixir of long life is powdered **mother of pearl**. The Chinese believe greatly in the auspicious attributes of this substance, and furniture that has mother of pearl decorations of *ling zhi herb* are said to add auspicious luck to the home.

The Queen of the West symbolizes all the aspirations of mankind

The Queen of the West is known as **Hsi Wang Mu**. She is often depicted with a retinue of five fairy attendants, usually seated on a peacock or phoenix and wearing an elaborate headdress. She is often depicted with a crane and also many types of birds. Doves served as her messengers. She had two main attendants, one carried a bowl of the peaches of immortality and the other carried a large fan. She lived in a palace with extensive gardens in the holy *Kunlun mountains*. In her manicured grounds within which grew many different kinds of magical plants was also the fabled fairy peach plants which blossom, bear fruit and ripen once every three thousand years. Anyone eating these peaches would be made immortal.

The Queen of the West is a very popular subject of paintings and screens, and her images are often accompanied with brilliantly written good fortune verses that are said to bring extreme good luck to households.

I displayed a relatively old **Hsi Wang Mu** screen in my home for fifteen years, and each time I entertained a feng shui master to lunch, he would comment extremely favourably on the screen. Every feng shui Master voiced loud approval and each offered me an interpretation of the auspicious Chinese characters that came with the screen. Later, I presented the screen as a marriage gift to the son of a good friend.

The Queen of the West symbolizes many good things including a long life filled with great honour, wealth, fame and recognition. She brings good and obedient sons into households. Families stay together and siblings enjoy relationships that are free of petty squabbling. She is best shown with all her fairy attendants, seated on a grand carriage drawn by phoenixes and peacocks. Screens that feature her are not difficult to find in Hong Kong, Taiwan and China. Place the screen near the vicinity of the main front door.

THE KUNLUN mountains is a legendary range of mountains said to be located somewhere in Central Asia near to or as part of the Himalayas. It has been compared to Mt. Kailash - said to be home of the Hindu Gods, as well as to Mount Meru, the holy Buddhist mountain where it is said gem trees grow in profusion.

Hang longevity calligraphy in your living room to create long life chi

The Chinese have always valued calligraphy, which is the art of skillfully painting characters with the Chinese brush such that the strength, stamina and intrinsic *chi* (or special life force energy) is successfully transferred onto paper. From a feng shui perspective, calligraphy represents the end result of good human *chi* in action, and this harmonizes with the *chi* of the environment to bring about good fortune. It is the work of the skilled artisan with the *kung fu* or expertise that has the ability to transfer good *chi* onto rice paper, in the form of characters. Calligraphy is thus considered a manifestation of good feng shui. When the characters that are written are also auspicious words, or words that connote different types of good fortune, it is even more auspicious.

Thus hanging stylish calligraphy is usually regarded as good feng shui.

One of the most popular words frequently rendered in calligraphy is the word that means *longevity*. Three versions of this word are illustrated here. The illustration here is not calligraphy; rather they are stylized versions of the word. Hopefully readers will be able to recognize this word when they come across it in other mediums of Chinese art, costume or decorative symbols. It is also good to look for calligraphy of this word and to hang such calligraphy in the bedroom of the patriarch.

All furniture carved with the longevity symbol are popular with the older folk. I strongly recommend placing these insignias onto dining tables, coffee tables, desks, beds and cupboards. Decorative ornamentation of furniture, complete with mother of pearl and auspicious longevity motif is shown on the cabinet below. Furniture like this is very popular with Chinese households, especially when the longevity sign is worked into the design of the decorative carving. This is because the essence of longevity is not merely long life, but also good health and plenty of harmony and happiness for the family.

The Three Star Gods or Fuk Luk Sau bring great good fortune

Much Taoist literature refer to the seven stars that make up the constellation which astronomers have named the Plough, the Great Bear and the Great Dipper of the northern skies. This constellation of seven stars are said to represent heavenly deities, each representing one aspect of good fortune. Of the seven however, three star Deities stand out prominently in the pantheon of good fortune symbols. These Deities represent the three most important manifestations of good fortune and they are collectively referred to as **Fuk Luk Sau.**

The **first star Deity** reflects the universal wish for long life and this is represented by the God of Longevity (**Sau**) carrying a staff with a bottle gourd of nectar. He is usually accompanied by a white crane amidst some pine branches. Sau is placed on the right as shown above.

The **second star Deity** is the God of Power (**Luk**). He represents the power of the high Government official and holds the *ru yi* or scepter of office in his left hand. The God of power always stands in the center.

The **third star Deity** reflects the universal wish for wealth and enhanced income. The God of Income and Prosperity (**Fuk**) wearing a red robe of a merchant and carrying a child represents this. Luk is placed on the left as shown in the picture above.

Together, the three star Gods are said to symbolize health, wealth and happiness. This is interpreted as longevity, prosperity and power! They should be placed on a high side table in the dining room from where they are said to create auspicious *chi* for the entire household. At the office, Fuk Luk Sau can be placed behind you, giving vital support and good fortune.

Chapter Three:
Symbols of Love & Romance

By combining Chinese astrology with the feng shui of the five elements, you can use potent symbols of romance to jazz up your love life, enhance your friendships, get an unwilling lover to commit and energize the conjugal happiness of your marriage. Discover the potency of **love symbols**.

Place a pair of **mandarin ducks** and watch them bring love back into a sagging marriage. Hang or display **beautiful peonies** to enhance romance in your special relationships; and wear the **double happiness** symbol for greater marriage joy. Discover a load of other significant signs which can be activated. Learn to use **lights**, display **crystals**, and wear specially designed stunning diamond **jewellery** to bring love into your life.

In FENG SHUI, love and romance always means the luck of having a happy marriage and family life that is blessed with many bright happy children, especially lots of sons to carry on the family name.

Thus all love energizers bring marriage opportunities to unmarried single men and women, and they enhance the love, commitment and loyalty between spouses. Using the symbols of conjugal happiness to activate romance luck always implies hoping for a permanent commitment. In the Chinese view of family, there is no suggestion of frivolous relationships. Marriages are regarded as sacred, and infidelities as we presently know it did not really exist.

Olden Chinese society was a polygamous society. Men frequently had multiple wives and concubines. As such, we have to be careful when choosing and displaying love symbols. It is necessary not to overdo the presence of these love symbols, in case they result in the men developing roving eyes. It is also necessary to take note of some simple safeguards to ensure that an outside third party does not come between the spouses in the marriage or relationship.

Before marriage, activating for love brings marriage opportunities, but it does not guarantee a permanent conjugal commitment between the couple. Thus feng shui can help attract marriage opportunities for men and women, but it cannot guarantee the quality of the mate! Also, it is useful to know that if the *marriage corner* happens to be occupied by a toilet, then displaying a love symbol inside the toilet could well attract a most unsuitable match, one which could bring bad luck to the relationship. Usually, the marriage and romance corner is the place of the matriarchal trigram *Kun* and this is the Southwest sector of any home. Use a compass to determine the Southwest location of the house. If this corner of the home is occupied by a toilet or is missing, marriage opportunities of single residents are seriously afflicted. Then look for the SW of the bedroom OR the Southwest of the living room to activate with love symbols. Do not do anything to activate the *chi* inside the toilet.

After marriage, connubial bliss between the spouses depends on their heaven luck or karma. However, their marriage karma can be greatly enhanced with a feng shui inspired display of symbols of family harmony. These should always include symbols that signify lots of sons, since this is presumed to be the main determinant of happiness.

Thus included in the selection of symbols in this section of the book will also be those that magnify family harmony, and those that ensure plenty of offsprings especially male offspring.

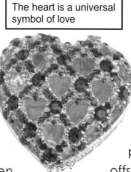

The heart is a universal symbol of love

Mandarin Ducks to create marriage opportunities

Mandarin ducks are the famous symbols of lovers. Placed as a pair, they create the kind of *chi* that is most conducive for lovers to become a married couple. In fact, a pair of mandarin ducks is probably the most potent symbol of married bliss. Anyone wanting to energize their love life should really go out and get an image of these ducks.

It would be best however to avoid ducks carved out of wood. This is because the use of wood clashes with the element that needs to be energized, which is earth. *Small wood* would not matter but carved mandarin ducks are usually made of *big wood* element (i.e. wood from big trees.) Because of this, I usually recommend to my single friends in search of love, to either display a painting of a pair of ducks, OR to find sculptures of mandarin ducks that are made of a semi precious stone.

This will magnify the earth element which in turn strongly activates the *Kun* trigram of the Southwest. The trigram *Kun* favours marriage. This trigram belongs to the SW sector, which is also the sector that signifies romance and marriage. So placing a pair of ducks in the SW sector of your living room, bedroom or home will activate love and marriage chi!

Of the semi-precious stones, the most potent would be ducks made of red jasper, red cornelian or red coral. Of the three, jasper is the least expensive and also the best. This is because the colour of jasper is extremely favourable for the SW corner. A second reason is that there are minute traces of iron in jasper, and this makes the stone itself a very powerful energizer. In fact, most auspicious symbols when fashioned out of jasper strongly magnifies their potency. This is especially the case for symbols that are suitable for the earth corners of the home.

Geese signify the togetherness of the married state

While the mandarin duck is said to symbolize conjugal fidelity, a pair of geese soaring high together signifies the happy togetherness of the married state. Thus while mandarin ducks are more suitable for those aspiring towards marriage and looking to enter into a relationship with a suitable mate, those already married should think of displaying a pair of geese instead.

A pair of geese holds out the promise of a marriage being gloriously happy with no separation between the spouses. If you are newly married and work tends to keep you both separated, go look for a screen with a pair of flying geese, or look for images of two flying geese to stick on the Southwest wall of your living room. They make for very happy relationships. These creatures have beautiful plumage and are said

Mandarin Ducks symbolize a long lasting marriage

to pine for their mates. They are supposedly so attached to each other that one will never fly without the other.

Geese are also said to symbolize the male yang energy so they are emblems of good fortune. In the winter, they instinctively fly south towards the source of warmth. Being a migratory bird, a goose signifies the spirit of adventure. But they never fly singly. They always fly in a pair, and as a marriage or betrothal gift, they symbolize wishes of togetherness for the happy couple. Geese are faithful creatures. They do not mate a second time. Due to this attribute, the goose is also a symbol of undying love. Those who stay true to the memory of their departed loved ones are said to personify the spirit of the goose.

Other birds that can take the place of both the mandarin ducks and the goose are the budgerigars or **lovebirds**. Some people refer to these birds as miniature parrots. They are called lovebirds because of their extreme attachment to their mates.

Budgerigars

These birds are rarely seen sitting alone. They move in pairs. If you are unable to get hold of the Chinese symbols, these western love birds would be excellent substitutes.

Whatever bird you use, please remember never to place them singly or alone or separated from their mate. And do not display more than a pair. If you place more than two birds, the relationship gets crowded and you would only be setting yourself up for heartbreak. Keep them in the Southwest either in the living area or in the bedroom and keep them well lit.

The double happiness sign is simply a "must" to ensure marriage luck

The Chinese have many symbols for signifying conjugal happiness. No matter which symbol you display in your home, however, happiness *chi* is most efficiently created by the word itself doubled. Thus the most powerful and widely recognized symbol of marital happiness is the *double happiness* sign. This sign is carved on marital beds, chairs and other bedroom furniture. It is also printed onto silks and brocades meant for wearing on the marriage day. In addition, invitation cards summoning guests to a wedding often had the double happiness sign prominently embossed into its design.

In a culture where superstition and social mores were scrupulously adhered to during the old days, the ritual of marriage was confined only to marriages contracted between a man and his first and principle wife. In the same way, therefore, the double happiness symbol could only be used to decorate the wedding furniture and festivities of the man's first marriage. All subsequent marriages to secondary wives were deemed undeserving of the epitaph "double happiness". This nonsense does not hold any credence now. I have used the double happiness symbol to decorate many pieces of my furniture, and I do it to create a harmonious flow of happy energy through my home. It is in the same vein and following the same logic that I decided to make a collection of double happiness rings, earrings and cufflinks for everyone to wear the imprint of *happiness doubled* on their bodies to simulate the potency of this wonderful symbol.

The double happiness calligraphy is also an excellent method of displaying the sign in the home. But do hang it in your bedroom and hang it on the wall sector that represents your personalized marriage corner based on the Eight Mansions or KUA formula*. This will successfully create excellent marriage happiness *chi* for you.

* The Eight Mansions or KUA formula offers personalized auspicious and inauspicious directions and sectors that are worked out based on your date of birth.

The *mou tan* or mountain peony for a wonderful love life

The peony is China's Queen of Flowers. It signifies beauty, romance and the amorous feelings of youth. The peony comes in a variety of stunning colours, but it is the **red peony** that symbolizes love and is usually the colour most admired and valued. If you hang a painting of red peonies in your home, it signifies you have beautiful and eligible daughters whose hand in marriage is still available.

Displaying peonies in the living room always benefits the young daughters of a family, as they are said to bring many suitors for their hands in marriage. The peony makes them witty and charming. Some say the legendary figure who is known as the **White Peony** was the pseudonym of a fairy creature so skilled in the arts of love she became a legend amongst those who pursued such pleasures. The beauty and lovemaking skills of the famous concubine **Yang Kuei Fei** was also likened to the peony.

Legend has it that she decorated her living quarters profusely with the mountain peony and that this kept the emperor's desire for her to continue unabated. The presence of the peonies acted like a love potion!

Displaying peonies in the bedroom is an enticement for a sexual (and sometimes illicit) entanglement. I always discourage married couples (those who have been married for a decade or more) from hanging paintings of the mountain peony in their bedroom. This will merely encourage the libido of the husband, causing him to look for "sweet young things" outside of the marriage.

A peony painting or vase of peonies should always be placed in the living room, and the motivation should be for it to benefit the daughters of the family and only those of marriageable age who are still staying with the family. Once they marry and leave the family home, it is advisable to remove the peony painting.

Butterflies are for those wanting an active social life without the commitment

The butterfly is a symbol of young love. This happy creature flits from flower to flower sipping sweet nectar from the blooms signifying a happy social life for the youthful. It is the happiness of a frivolous sort, suggesting a period of a young person's life when it is not yet time for

marriage. Some say, therefore, that the butterfly symbolizes love that is not serious.

Butterflies generally connote young men with a flirtatious nature and are suitable for those who want to create the feng shui of an active social life, but who are not yet ready to make a commitment. Use of this symbol is therefore not very suitable for women, since it connotes a situation where there is little romance and plenty of fun - a situation more traditionally suited, it would seem, to the male than the female.

According to legend however, the butterfly signifies an *undying bond between lovers*. There is told the story of two young lovers, one a scholar, the other the daughter of a rich magistrate. The lovers met, fell in love and then were forced to separate by her parents. Heartbroken, the lovers die and in death are reunited. They reincarnate as two butterflies and as butterflies, the two are together forever!

As a result of this famous legend of star-crossed lovers, there are those who maintain that butterflies symbolize eternal love, not frivolous love. The romantics at heart would benefit hugely from placing the image of a pair of butterflies in the SW corner of the home.

If you are one of those who like butterflies and wish to display them in your home, I will have to say that butterflies that have been preserved and are displayed "pinned" down to a wooden board, emit quite a lot of yin energy. Butterflies like these are sold as tourist souvenirs, but these are actually the *corpses* of butterflies. They represent death because they really are dead butterflies, and I would say that this is not a good idea at all.

It is far better to hang a picture of auspicious flowers with butterflies as part of the picture. This also introduces the concept of *life,* and the flying butterfly then emits *yang* rather than yin energy.

The *lute* - a stringed musical instrument that signifies matrimonial happiness

Chinese string instruments (referred to as lutes) are believed to go as far back in history as to the time of **Fu Hsi,** the legendary emperor who was also the founder and first author of the I-Ching. These lutes are seven string and 25 string instruments known as **Ch'in** and **Se'.** These instruments are said to produce sounds so harmonious they signify the state of perfect union between a married couple. They are thus emblematic of matrimonial happiness.

These sounds supposedly express not merely the sexual bliss of matrimony, but more importantly, also exemplify the friendship between the Patriarch and the Matriarch. Both purity and moderation are invoked by the sweet sounds of the lutes, as a result of which the instruments themselves came to symbolize harmony and happiness in family life. The sounds of the **Ch'in** are said to create harmony while those of the

Se' are said to evoke gentle restraints that remind one of the amiable singing of pine trees. These are the sounds of happiness that produce thoughts of fidelity.

Traditional lutes of ancient times were reputed to have been made of wood from the Phoenix tree. Ritual soaking of the wood used and the measurements taken often accompanied the production of lutes. Originally, the lute had five strings, which emitted five notes, and this corresponded to the five elements. Later, this was extended to seven strings.

The lute is actually credited as having eight attributes, namely, happiness, elegance, sweetness, subtlety, nostalgia, softness, resonance and strength. These are qualities that describe matrimonial and family happiness. If you hang a painting which has a woman playing this musical instrument, the vibes created will be most beneficial.

In recent times, the flute has also come to be regarded as similarly auspicious for marital harmony. Thus, paintings of Chinese flute players dressed in traditional silks and brocades have become popular. In this context, the magnificent paintings of **Chen Yi Fei** are especially suitable.

I cannot afford Chen's paintings, but there are many Chinese oil painters who have taken their cue from Chen and started painting musical instruments being played by beautiful maidens. Displaying paintings like these in your living room would be most auspicious.

The Magpie is the bird of joy and of good omen

The sacred magpie features strongly in old Manchu legends that relate to its defeat of the Ming rulers and the founding of its dynastic rule over China. The Manchus thus regarded it as a magical bird for many centuries. The literal translation of the magpie is *bird of joy* and it is popularly believed that when the magpie nests in your house, it brings much cause for celebration and many *happy occasions*. Those wishing to settle down will find the opportunity to do so. Those wanting love and marriage will find it. And those wishing to have children will also be successful. It creates many *hei see* or happy occasions. In addition to being a bringer of joy, the magpie is also considered to be a bird of good omen.

When you are fantasizing on a plan to get rich, or thinking through a strategy for getting a new job, or starting a new venture - and if you were to suddenly see a magpie - it is said to be a sign that you will succeed in attaining your goals. It is therefore a good idea to have either an image or a painting of a magpie in your home. This means success for all your plans.

The magpie looks a little bit like the crow, except that it is smaller and has a snowy white patch under its body. In Malaysia, the magpie is more brown than black and it also has some white markings near its beak. It is possible to teach the magpie to talk, if you are patient enough.

However, just because it is a bird of good omen, do not keep the magpie in captivity. **Do not keep any bird in captivity** since this creates inauspicious chi for the home. It is extremely unlucky to keep caged birds, since this symbolizes an inability to fly. This sort of *chi* is afflicted and seriously limits your ability to grow, develop and move upwards in your career. Other lucky birds whose images are said to be auspicious are the rooster, the peacock, the flamingo, the mandarin duck, the goose or the crane. Images of any of these birds in the South sector of your home bring family harmony.

Paper Lanterns with auspicious characters are symbols of fertility

There are many beautiful stories that describe the way lanterns cast auspicious light on humble abodes enhancing the living space and bringing occasions of great joy to families. Lanterns written with auspicious characters or decorated with beautiful symbols have always been regarded as emblems of fertility. Thus, to enhance the speedy conception of a child, lamps were often strategically placed under the bridal bed. Such lamps were named Children and Grandchildren Lamps.

Sometimes, two red lanterns were hung, one on each side for the bride and groom, by the side of the bridal bed. These lamps were lit together and if they burned at the same rate, going out at the same time, it was regarded as an auspicious sign indicating a long and happy marriage.

Such lanterns would often have the auspicious double happiness word printed onto the lamp, and these came in various designs. These lanterns were believed to attract the precious yang chi that often caused conception leading to the birth of a son. When the wife became pregnant, the lamp continued to be lit each night.

Lanterns are generally considered to be such auspicious symbols that a special day was set aside each year to celebrate the lantern festival. This is the fifteenth day of the first Chinese month and it coincided with the last day of the lunar New year celebrations. A second lantern festival is held on the 7**th** day of the 7**th** moon during which time the *7 beautiful sisters of heaven* would descend onto earth. My mother used to tell me that on this night, the 7 sisters would pass by homes with lanterns and drop a little of their *magical moon powder* which would mingle with the ash from special fragrant joss sticks burned at altars for that occasion. Such magical moon powder was said to enhance the beauty of unmarried maidens, thereby assisting them to attract handsome husbands!

To attract the 7 heavenly sisters into the home, lanterns such as the ones shown here would be hung by the entrance door into the home.

Invoke the God of marriage and use bright vermilion lights for romance

The **Chinese God of Marriage** (yes, there is a God of Marriage, so all you singles take heart!) is called **Chieh Lin** and he is none other than *the old man on the moon*. He is believed to be in charge of all nuptials between mortals, and he reportedly sanctions unions between potential couples on earth by symbolically tying their feet together with an invisible red silk cord.

This belief provided the origin for the bride and groom at Chinese weddings sealing their marriage pledge to each other by drinking wine from two glasses that are tied together with red cord. To activate romance luck in your home therefore, it is an excellent idea to display a painting of the full moon. Such an image actually signifies *yang in yin* and during the 15th of each month this becomes a most auspicious time for undertaking

all projects that relate to matters of the heart. I was also told that placing the *old man in the moon* in the SW corner of the house was most auspicious for romance. However, while I may have heard references to this God of Marriage, I myself have never seen an image of him, so apart from knowing who and what he is, I am unable to offer a visual despite much research on the matter.

A more down to earth and practical suggestion is to use a lot of vermilion red in the SW to jazz up the fire energy of this corner. As any Chinese knows, red has always been the colour of happiness and joy. Thus to energize romance and marriage luck, introduce curtains, wallpaper and carpets that are strong on vermilion.

The vermilion red of fire produces earth in the productive cycle of element relationships, and this, together with the strong presence of *yang,* should successfully activate the SW. Do all this in the living room of your home and not your bedroom. When there is too much *yang* energy in the bedroom, you will find it difficult to have a good nights sleep.

If you prefer, it works equally well to install bright lights in the SW of the living area instead of going red there. Lights also suggest yang energy and lights are also an excellent method of activating the earth energy of the sector. Turn on the light for at least three hours each evening. In feng shui, fire energy is always a powerful energizer. It is only necessary to remember never to overdo it with too much light, and secondly, to understand that lights are not so good for the NW and West sectors.

The Dragon for good descendants luck and the wish for many sons

One of the *rituals* at marriage celebrations during the old days was the dragon dance, which was held to invoke descendants' luck - the issue of many sons to carry on the family name. Indeed, a great deal of marriage and good fortune rituals associated with wedlock is connected to the wish for sons, and wealthy families frequently went to great lengths to ensure that the feng shui of the family mansion took this aspiration into account.

One custom which seems to have lost its appeal in the light of modern attitudes used to require the bride, upon entering her husband's household for the first time, to be carried over a pan of red hot burning charcoal. This would be laid on the threshold of the door, and the bride would have to be carried by two women whose husbands and children were still alive. This ritual was to ensure the bride would be successful in childbirth, and that there would be no complications that might cause her to die in childbirth.

Up in the bridal chamber, the family matriarch would have arranged for a young virgin boy born in the year of the dragon to roll on the bridal bed three times to activate *yang* energy for the couple. Lanterns would have been hung with the double happiness words and the bridal curtain would have been embroidered with the image of many children. These rituals were to ensure a fruitful union that results in children. Most important would be the presence of the dragon image in the home, preferably images of the nine

dragons since this reflected the sons of the dragon.

The image above of the dragon with a pearl can be placed in the bedroom during child bearing years to ensure many sons!

When seeking life partners ensure yin yang balance at home

It is a generally known fact that good feng shui is all about balancing yin and yang forces in the living space. What is less obvious is how this is interpreted and applied. How does the amateur practitioner know which object is yin and which object is yang? How does one succeed in getting just the correct balance?

The standard list of yin and yang objects is straightforward enough. Thus the sun, noise, white, red, yellow, odd numbers, male, light, heaven, fire, heat, positive forces and all matter with life represent the **yang force**. The moon, silence, black, darkness, female, stillness, even numbers, earth, water, cold, negative forces, ice, and death represent the **yin force**.

In feng shui orientations, it gets a little bit complex. Raised landforms (mountains) are yang, but a range of ridged landforms is said to be yin. Valleys and rivers are said to be yin, but they are also said to possess yang qualities when people settle in the valley and a town gets built. Yin and yang are constantly changing forces. The interplay of these primordial forces is always dynamic and changing, never static. This principle must be applied to the feng shui around the home. A useful guideline is to have structures, designs, and objects that seem to be opposite in attributes. Thus land levels should be both flat and raised. There should be light and water, and a profusion of colours. There should be sunlight and shade, and there should also be moonlight!

Inside, homes must also have both yin and yang forces. When a home is excessively yang, the male energy is deemed to be strong and powerful. Such a home lacks the matriarchal energy that brings hidden support and growth as a family. A home is said to suffer from too much *yang* when the colours of the home, from walls to floors are excessively red, when lights are excessively bright, when everything in the home suggests the male energy and when there is too high a noise level. This creates imbalance.

Homes that are excessively yin are usually not well-lit. Walls are dark and décor is somber. There is insufficient life in the house. Also, when the female energy is too strong, the house is too yin. Such homes usually have a hard time attracting good feng shui. There is a lack of family luck. Singles living in such homes have difficulty finding husbands or wives, or even of having a good social life.

If you are a single woman, magnify the yang male energy of your home

Single women living alone and looking for love and marriage should make real efforts to strengthen the male yang energy of their homes. One way of doing this is to make sure the home is well-lit. There should be a bright lamp in the SW corners both of the living room and of the bedroom. All the decorative art hung in the home should also reflect strong male energy.

Hang pictures of male heroes, male movie stars, male singing groups, even pictures of emperors (the one shown on the left is the Kangsi emperor of the Ching dynasty) – in fact just about any kind of illustrations, paintings or photographs that most fully represent your idea of the perfect man set against the kind of lifestyle and background you like. Just remember not to make your walls too yang.

Occasionally, displaying art that suggest love and romance with there being a couple in the picture would represent a balancing of the energies. Let there be lots of music in the house, since this brings in good life energy, and keep things in pairs to balance the decorative display. Avoid anything excessively yin in your decoration - so avoid dark colours. The minimalist look is not recommended. Neither are the rice coloured Japanese shades, since these suggest yin *chi*. Black furniture or carpets should always be balanced with strong lighting. Not strong as in harsh bright lights, but strong as in having the room well-lit.

To be on the safe side, implement these energizing ideas in your living room and never in your bedroom. You must guard

against making your bedroom too *yang*, since this makes you far too aggressive in your search; the *chi* that emanates from you will be too powerful, thereby driving the men away!

For instance, do not paint your bedroom red. Nor should you display dragons in your bedroom if you are still unmarried. Remember that in the principle of yin and yang, the female is usually passive and yielding, not aggressive.

Thus you may be a very successful corporate-type woman, but if you are looking for a husband, it is a good idea to apply the principles of yin and yang. While you activate yang energies in the home, remember that your own personal feng shui should reflect the female yin principle.

If you are a bachelor activate yin energy in your home

Bachelors who want to settle down but simply cannot find the right girl might wish to undertake a feng shui analysis of their bachelor pads. Usually, their living space is very yang male, and the female *chi* is missing or in short supply. I have seen bachelor apartments that do not have objects that represent the female energy. Pictures on walls depict ships, guns, military or naval heroes. Items on the desk - all executive toys are male oriented. Things like paperweights, briefcases, ashtrays and cigarette boxes were usually made of materials and designed to be strongly suggestive of macho manly taste! Their living space also reflects the same excess of *yang* energies.

To attract in the womanly presence, the best thing you can do is to introduce female energy. Symbols associated with female energy are sculptures, portraits and paintings of women. It is an excellent idea to hang art work that depict the female form. Do not display antique paintings of women. You should also not hang old paintings that portray scenes from the old Chinese classics such as the *Dream of the Red Chamber,* since the women depicted in many of these stories are not women you would want to marry. Many are *foxes – spirit women –* who entice men for their temporary enjoyment. Recall also the legend of the white snake who transformed itself into a beautiful woman to snare the unsuspecting student. When hanging art

to get feng shui benefits, new art is always better than old art, unless you know the exact provenance of old pieces. It is the same with furniture.

There should be the symbolic presence of flowers that signify beautiful women or romance. The best flowers to display are **peonies,** which are powerful emblems of conjugal love. There are also flowers that signify married couples. These are the **narcissus** (which is also an excellent energizer for careers when displayed during the lunar New Year period), the **plum blossom**, and the **orchid**. A picture showing the narcissus and peony together signifies an impending marriage, while orchids and peonies symbolize a discovery of romance between two people whose families are close friends.

Peonies

I knew a bachelor in his fifties who had been sleeping on an antique bed carved with dragons and mother of pearl design for over twenty years. He was a very successful professional with his own firm. He had a lot of money, but his love and family life were totally non existent until for some reason he gave the bed away when he moved to a new penthouse. Within six months he met a lady friend, within a year this confirmed bachelor was married. Moral of story? Change your bed!

Crystals for magnifying romance luck in the SW corner

The picture here is a three inch high citrine crystal - slightly yellow in colour and filled with stunning occlusions. It has been my personal crystal for well over ten years now. It is what I call a natural crystal in that it came from the ground and is not man-made from sand and lead. It has been cut at the base so it is a single pointed crystal. I have always used this crystal to achieve various feng shui objectives. Usually, it is placed on the SW of my immediate space. Thus when it stands on my desk here at home, it will be on the SW corner of my desk. This energizes my matriarchal luck. When I feel like having a more active social life, I place this citrine on my desktop.

Since I am not looking for romance, I do not use this crystal to energize romance luck and so I do not place it in my bedroom. However, by merely being in the SW corner of my work area (where I spend most of my time when I am at home) the crystal causes the earth luck of the SW to bring me a good and harmonious family life. To those who are single, using this kind of crystal to energize the SW of your bedroom will be excellent for activating romance, love and marriage opportunities. Place it preferably as near the bed as possible.

You can also use quartz or amethyst crystals if you wish, and if you like, you can have them as smooth pebbles. If you place them with a growing plant, it is best that you put it into your living room and not the bedroom.

Smooth crystal balls are also wonderful energizers, and in fact are better than pebbles.

Crystal balls are excellent for **relationship luck**. They are also excellent for **networking luck**, to attract powerful people into your life. To activate this kind of luck, you should have **six crystal balls.** They do not all need to be of the same size, but they should ideally be in the Northwest sector of the living room.

Learn the KUA number formula to discover your *love mansion* direction

In addition to energizing the SW corner of your home and bedroom for romance and marriage luck, anyone wanting to improve a serious relationship (be it in a marriage or in any other kind of relationship) should learn about the KUA formula. This is part of *"Eight Mansions Compass Formula of Feng Shui"* and is extremely powerful in activating different types of luck, including marriage and romance luck. First, you should learn how to determine your individual KUA number.

The formula for determining your KUA number.

Using your *lunar** calendar year of birth, add the last two digits. Keep adding the digits until you get a single digit number. Then:

For MEN: Deduct this number from 10, if you were born before 2000, deduct from 9, for those born in the year 2000 or after. The result is your KUA number.

For WOMEN: Add this number to 5, if you were born before 2000, add to 6, for those born in the year 2000 and after. The result is your **KUA** number. If you get two digits, keep adding until you reduce it to one digit e.g. if you get the number 10 then 1+0=1; and if you get the number 14 then 1+4=5.

EXAMPLE 1: If you were born on the 28th August 1957, then adding 5+7=12 and then adding 1+2=3. Next for men, it will be 10-3=7 so the KUA is **7.** For women it will be 3+5=8 so the KUA is **8**

EXAMPLE 2: If you were born on the 2nd January 1962, then because this date is before the lunar new year, you must deduct 1 from the year of birth. You must use 1961. So to calculate your KUA number, you take 6+1=7. Then for men, 10-7=3 so the KUA is **3.**

For women, 7+5=12 and then 1+2=3 so the KUA is also **3.** To energize your *love mansion,* you should take note of where it is. Your love mansion is where your **nien yen** location is. For this, check the table below:

Your KUA number	Your **nien yen** location	The element to energize
1 (East group)	South	Fire and Wood
2 (West group)	Northwest	Metal and Earth
3 (East group)	Southeast	Wood and Water
4 (East group)	East	Wood and Water
5 (West group)	Northwest for males; West for females	Metal and Earth
6 (West group)	Southwest	Earth and Fire
7 (West group)	Northeast	Earth and Fire
8 (West group)	West	Metal and Earth
9 (East group)	North	Water and Metal

* *this means if you were born before the Lunar New Year in each year, you must deduct 1 from your year of birth (you need the **date** of birth to determine this since generally, this affects those born before February 4th but it is useful to check a Lunar calendar to be exact).*

Energize your nien yen or *love mansion* with special symbols

Different people should energize different corners of their homes to activate their respective personalized *love mansion* location. This is in addition to the general SW location, which enhances relationship luck for everyone in the home. The SW benefits everyone because it is the place of the *Kun* trigram, which indicates the luck of love and romance, as well as the luck of the family staying as a cohesive unit.

To augment this, those who are single or whose marriages could do with a bit of feng shui help should check the table in the preceding page and discover where their *personalized love mansion* is, based on their KUA numbers. Generally, it is best to energize the corners of the living room rather than the bedroom.

6 Rod Metal Windchime

Those with KUA number 1 should energize the **South** wall and corner of their home. The elements to activate are fire and wood. Here are three suggestions:

• Paint the South wall yellow, white or red.

• Hang a red coloured double happiness lantern.

• Place a pair of mandarin ducks or geese in the South corner. For opportunities to find love, display the celestial phoenix. If you are a woman, display the male yang phoenix, which is more colourful; if you are a man, place a female yin phoenix. Or place a dragon and phoenix together.

Those with KUA number 2 should activate the **Northwest** wall or corner of their home. The elements to magnify are metal and earth. Here are three suggestions:

• Hang a metal windchime with 6 rods.

• Paint the NW wall a metallic colour.

• Have a brass or ceramic vase in the NW corner.

Those with KUA number 3 should activate the **Southeast** corner or wall, and the elements to energize would be wood and water. Some suggestions would include the following:

- Place a deep and wide brimmed bowl of water and grow a small green plant in this water. Keep the water clean and the plant healthy.

- Keep a pair of goldfish with bubbling oxygenators in a small aquarium.

- Display a big vase full of silk peonies - red or pink.

Don't overdo things. One energizing symbol is enough to get the *chi* flowing

Those with KUA number 4 should activate the **East** wall or corner of their home. The elements to magnify are big wood and water. Suggestions:

- Display a healthy, flowering plant.

- Display the dragon image.

- Display a jade decorative piece.

Those with KUA number 5 should activate the **Northwest** corner or wall for men, and the **West** wall for women. The elements to energize would be metal and earth. Some suggestions would include the following:

- Display a 6 or 7 rod windchime.

- Place six crystal balls in the NW and 7 in the West.

- Place a moon symbol.

Those with KUA number 6 should activate the **Southwest** wall or corner of their home. The elements to magnify are earth and fire. Suggestions:

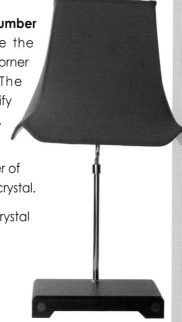

- Display a cluster of natural quartz crystal.

- Hang a small crystal chandelier.

- Display a lamp with a bright vermilion red lampshade.

Those with KUA number 7 should activate the **Northeast** wall or corner of their home. The elements to magnify are earth and fire and the suggestions would be similar as for KUA number 6. **Those with KUA number 8** should activate the **West** wall or corner of their home. The elements to magnify are metal and earth and are similar as for KUA number 5.

Those with KUA number 9 should activate the **North** wall or corner of their home. The elements to magnify are water and metal. Suggestions:

- A brightly lit aquarium with many fast swimming fish (guppies or goldfish).

- A metal vase with auspicious designs.

- A painting of water scenery.

Symbols of love need not be Chinese. Anything that suggests love creates the *chi*

It is a mistake to think that only Chinese symbols work. You can look for symbols of romance from your own personal culture.

Symbolism in feng shui has to do with the quality of energy, and the stronger the belief systems, usually the stronger will be the energies created. For this reason, I am not surprised when feng shui experts suggest red hearts and western love birds in place of double happiness and phoenix symbols when asked to energize the romance luck for their clients.

In this connection, some of the most powerful symbols of love would be the prints of romantic paintings. By this, I do not mean sexually charged paintings, but rather those that suggest either conjugal love or family happiness. Thus I have always loved **Gustav Klimpt's "The Kiss"** – a stunning painting with awesome power to suggest intense and exciting romance. When you come across any painting that seems to move you with its romanticism, do get it and hang it in your home. Remember, different people find different things romantic!

Another powerful energizer of *love chi* that was *invented* by the West is the crystal chandelier which itself, is also an excellent feng shui symbol, because it signifies the yang energy of earth come alive. If you cannot afford something as elaborate as the one shown above, look for smaller substitutes. They can be quite affordable.

Remember that when you energize for love, you will yourself be the most powerful enhancer of the energies of your space. Many people forget this is one of the things that make symbolic feng shui work so well. The human psyche energizes strongly through our own belief systems.

By understanding the basis of the symbolic meanings that lie behind objects, we empower the objects with positive accumulations of chi energy. This when applied with proper understanding of the five elements (or *wu xing*) in turn attracts into our world wonderful happiness luck. So when energizing for romance, do not be afraid to allow room for your own creativity to show through!

Chapter Four:
Auspicious Rituals for
Marriages & Birthdays

I f you wish, you can observe good fortune rituals associated with marriage, birthdays and other *hei see* or happy occasions that mark the turning points of one's life. Many of these rituals border on superstition and incorporate feng shui symbols that add meaning and colour to

the celebratory occasions of life, Chinese style. These rituals (and taboos) reflect the rich symbolism of the Chinese tradition underlying which is the desire to ensure that happy occasions are celebrated in a way that attracts a continious flow of good fortune. Understanding these rituals will complement much of the practice of everyday feng shui. This auspicious image here depicts the Three Star Gods: Fuk, Luk and Sau – the Gods who stand for Health, Wealth and Happiness. Children holding good fortune symbols represent descendents luck. The peach signifies longevity, while the ru yi is the symbol of authority.

Checking the compatibility of couples from their horoscopes

The Chinese have a beautiful belief about couples being preordained from birth to marry each other. One of the legends goes that the God of Marriage, the old man in the moon, pairs off young girls and boys at birth by tying invisible red silk threads onto their toes. When they grow up and meet, they will be powerfully drawn to each other and a marriage between them is the definite outcome. They will also be astrologically well suited to each other.

However, not all couples that are meant for each other this way succeed in meeting. Sometimes invisible chi forces create obstacles that stand in the way of their ever meeting. To overcome these obstacles, it is a good idea to use all the methods given in the previous chapter to activate and enhance marriage luck. And to ensure that any impending match will be successful, casting the marriage horoscope would be an excellent idea. In the old days, marriages amongst the children of powerful and rich families were never left to chance, since matchmakers would have worked closely with parents to arrange suitable matches. Suitability was based on the respective horoscopes of the couple. Marriage horoscopes were part of elaborate rituals performed prior to there being a marriage.

In today's world, even if we have done away with the matchmaker, checking the horoscope surely cannot hurt. See what the stars say about the couple.

I strongly recommend that the 8 character charts of the couple be examined to ensure compatibility. These can be bought off internet websites that offer Four Pillar and 8 Character readings. They have programs that have computerized the calculations, thereby making it easy to get these horoscope charts cast.

These charts reveal the *weighting* of the five elements and using the Productive and Destructive cycle of elements, you can see immediately if two people are compatible. Better than the internet is to go to a professional expert on the Four Pillars and Eight Characters. If you find all this too tedious, then I suggest you at least undertake a reading based on the earthly branches ie on the animal years under which the couple were born.

These animal sign readings may appear superficial but are remarkably accurate in categorizing general compatibility.

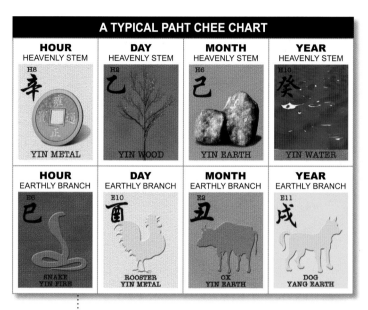

A TYPICAL PAHT CHEE CHART			
HOUR HEAVENLY STEM	**DAY** HEAVENLY STEM	**MONTH** HEAVENLY STEM	**YEAR** HEAVENLY STEM
H8 辛 YIN METAL	H2 乙 YIN WOOD	H6 己 YIN EARTH	H10 癸 YIN WATER
HOUR EARTHLY BRANCH	**DAY** EARTHLY BRANCH	**MONTH** EARTHLY BRANCH	**YEAR** EARTHLY BRANCH
E6 巳 SNAKE YIN FIRE	E10 酉 ROOSTER YIN METAL	E2 丑 OX YIN EARTH	E11 戌 DOG YANG EARTH

Antidotes for horoscope incompatibility between couples

My daughter who has just read the preceding page asks me "*what happens if the horoscope chart indicates incompatibility between the couple?*" I told her that I would then recommend a second reading by another expert, much like getting a second doctor's opinion on a diagnosis, and if that too came out negative, I would suggest that the couple do not proceed into marriage.

Jennifer finds it incredulous that I would recommend and accept this and walks off in something of a huff, which set me thinking. There will be amongst my readers young people whose romantic view of relationships preclude bad signs and bad horoscope incompatibilities - such a pity since problems will inevitably arise later on in a marriage between two wholly incompatible people. Can feng shui mitigate such a situation?

I believe so. According to feng shui masters, incompatibility between two people that are based on birth charts can be appeased by having *marriage harmony symbols* in the bridal bedroom, and also by the *correct exchange of gifts* between the bride and groom during the marriage ceremonials.

Marriage harmony symbols

The best of these symbols are the double happiness sign and the pair of *mandarin ducks or geese*. Have these symbols carved onto beds and bedroom furniture. Two ducks for instance can be sketched as

a carving on an antique marriage bed. Likewise, geese and ducks - emblems of marital harmony - can also be carved onto bedroom furniture.

The *double happiness sign* is the other powerful emblem of conjugal harmony. Have it nearby, either drawn as calligraphy or worn as a wedding ring. This ensures there is harmony between the couple and that it will be long lasting. It is also excellent for the couple to sleep with their heads pointed to the **nien yen** direction (check out the 8 mansions KUA formula). Amongst other auspicious outcomes of doing this, creating harmony between them is one. If the **nien yen** directions of the couple differ, as they definitely will if they are incompatible, the husband's direction should be used. This is because it is the husband's luck that will influence the state of the marriage.

The exchange of gifts expresses good wishes that bring good luck

A correct exchange of gifts based on the practice of symbolic feng shui can help mitigate some of the obstacles represented by incompatible horoscope charts. Usually the source of the incompatibility is due to a clashing of the five elements. Thus if the horoscope of the bride lacks the element of *water*, and that of the bridegroom has an excess of earth, then because earth destroys water, the marriage will cause the bride to die of thirst (joke) through lack of water. A gift that suggests the water element from the bridegroom at the time of marriage symbolizes that with the marriage, things will improve for her. The gift would make things more harmonious between them. It would be wonderful then if the bridegroom gave his wife a pair of blue shoes, a black evening dress, blue sapphire earrings, blue eye shadow, a set of blue bed sheets and a pair of goldfish in a small aquarium. All these suggestions manifest the water element and would be suitable when there is a lack of water in the horoscope chart. The bride can undertake the same analysis when selecting gifts for her husband. Gifts such as these recommended are not the traditional good fortune gifts given as part of the marriage ritual. They are modern day adaptations based on the theory and method of *wu xing* or **five element compensation.**

Suggestions for the other four elements are:

To compensate for *a lack of fire*, give red outfits, rubies, coral, garnets or cornelians, chandeliers and lights. To compensate for *a lack of earth*, give all kinds of semi precious gemstones and crystal. To compensate for *a lack of wood*, give silk flowers, paintings of auspicious flowers and healthy leafy plants. To compensate for *a lack of metal*, give plenty of gold.

According to the **Book of Rites**, the exchange of gifts is to express mutual wishes for fidelity, protection and the successful procreation of children from the union. An auspicious number of gifts is eight. The bridegroom should send eight gifts amongst which should be:

- a piece of gold jewellery for her hair as this will be auspicious
- a gilt mirror to protect her from bad *chi* and evil spirits
- a box of chocolates or sweetmeats to wish her a sweet life
- a length of red brocade or silk for her material happiness
- a gift of money (coins & notes) for her brothers and parents
- a painting with child & fish to signify successful childbirth
- a bunch of peonies (can be made of silk) for marital happiness
- a sandalwood fan to signify she will have his protection all her life

It is most auspicious for brides to wear the *qua* or ceremonial wedding dress

In Chinese weddings, the bride is usually elaborately made up and dressed in a red *qua*. This is the ceremonial wedding dress and is usually decorated with beads, crystals and sometimes even precious stones. The qua would have elaborate embroidery which features the auspicious dragon and phoenix or peonies and other symbols of good fortune. Wearing the *qua* ceremonial wedding dress is very significant and auspicious for the couple, especially for the bride. Only the first wife is entitled to wear the *qua*. This signifies her new status in life.

I strongly advise Chinese brides, no matter how modern you are, to get married in a *qua*, since it is most auspicious to do so. You can buy exceptionally beautiful *quas* literally off the peg in the Chinese Arts and Crafts department stores of Kowloon in Hong Kong. Do not buy a *qua* until you have definite marriage plans. An old wives tale suggests that to buy a *qua* prematurely or to buy a marriage bed prematurely causes bad luck that negates your chances of getting married. So do not buy an antique wedding bed for your unmarried daughters!

If you do not want a qua, at least get married in **red**. Do not wear black, since this is much too *yin* for what should be a *yang* occasion. It could cause a senior relative (like a father or an uncle) who is attending the celebrations to succumb to serious illness that could prove fatal. The Chinese refer to this as being seriously affected by the yin energy emanated. Remember that the bride must not wear black at her own wedding. (I have attended weddings where the bride actually comes out in a black evening dress in one of

The *Qua*, or ceremonial wedding dress, for the Bride

her many changes of outfits!) Guests should also not wear black to a wedding, as this is deemed to be very unkind. They may however wear red, since this heightens the yang energy.

Later, the bride attends a reception dinner where food is served and the marriage is celebrated. On the food table, there should be many auspicious objects. This can be the dragon phoenix pair or the double happiness symbol. The bride and groom then drink a mixture of wine and honey out of glasses tied together with **red** thread, exchanging goblets and then drinking again. This seals their commitment to each other. The bride then changes out of her heavy ceremonial bridal *qua* dress into a more comfortable evening *cheong sam* which should also be **red** in colour.

Get married in a red car decorated with auspicious symbols

In the old days, the groom's party would come and collect the bride in a red marriage sedan chair that would be elaborately decorated with auspicious symbols like lanterns and firecrackers. In this day and age, the sedan chair is outdated, but the red colour continues to have it's significance. Thus it is a good idea to get married in a red car. If this proves difficult, I recommend that some effort at least be

made to decorate the car with auspicious symbols. Thus use red satin ribbons to tie an endless knot that symbolizes eternal love, or use a double happiness decal to decorate the two sides of the car.

Marriage celebrations in the old days often started with a procession of the bride going to the groom's house. The bridal sedan chair would have the family name of the groom emblazoned in red characters, and for luck, a bright red umbrella is borne aloft at the front of the procession by family retainers or relatives. In addition, numerous red satin and paper scrolls were carried as placards containing the double happiness characters in gilt to attract good fortune for the happy occasion. The bride's brothers walk near her chair while inside; her face is hidden by elaborate ceremonial headgear. Firecrackers are let off when the procession arrives at the groom's home.

When the bride descends from the chair, the youngest son of the groom's family greets her by holding a mirror towards her. But the bride must look down and an elderly lady and attendants would then lead her to the bridal chamber.

The rituals associated with the procession and arrival of bride at the groom's home – then letting of the fire crackers and the display of auspicious symbols – symbolize the loud celebration of a *hei see*, a happy occasion. Observing these rituals is believed to attract good *chi* that ensures the safe arrival of the bride to the groom's home, and further ensures that she will be happy as a new daughter to the husband's family. This means that the bride will live harmoniously with the in-laws. The red umbrella signifies that her new family will protect her. Her brothers walking along side her symbolizes her leaving her old family amicably and the gifts she brings with her (gold, jewellery, money and brocades) symbolize that she brings auspicious good fortune to her husband and his family.

The tea ceremony to family elders is rich with good meanings

To the Chinese, drinking tea is a symbol of eternal wakefulness and alertness. The story derives from an ancient fairy tale that involves **Tat Mo,** the Indian Brahmin generally credited with bringing Buddhism to China. He is also said to be the originator of the tea plant. Legend has it that one day, while meditating, sleep overcame him and he dozed off. When he awoke he was determined that it would never happen again, so he cut off his eyelids. These fell to the earth, took root, immediately sprouted and became the first tea plant. This is why, the elders say, drinking tea keeps one awake and fully alert!

Of course there are many varieties of tea - from the cooling green teas to the fragrant jasmine teas to the rich black teas. Amongst Asian cultures, both the Japanese and the Chinese have raised the drinking of tea to an extremely high art form. Drinking tea is a very elaborate production full of protocol and replete with symbolic meanings. Special utensils and teapots were used. Special varieties of teas were drunk differently, and special rituals accompanied the drinking of tea.

A most important tea drinking ritual is associated with marriage ceremonials. Newly married couples, dressed in their wedding finery, would kneel in front of their respective parents and each offer a small cup of tea after which the parents would bless them and offer them a red packet filled with money. The tea offering signifies respect for the parents and was an expression of filial gratitude.

According to custom, the more refined the variety of tea, the more substantial was the offering, and likewise the bigger the red packet in terms of money gift, the more auspicious would be the start of married life. In the old days, parents of the bride often presented gold to their departing daughter after the performance of the tea ceremony. This was deemed to be an auspicious offering although in modern times this offering has been replaced with a red packet of cash. Tea must also be offered to every member of the family one generation above the couple as an indication of respect to family elders.

Do not do away with this tea ceremony no matter how modern you are, because the tea ceremony brings good luck to you!

Auspicious first month ceremonials to elebrate the birth of sons

In terms of life aspirations, the birth of sons are always regarded as extremely happy occasions and there are specific customs and rituals that take place to commemorate the occasion. Especially amongst the rich and powerful, sons were deemed particularly important to carry on the family name. Girls were regarded as less important since they were expected eventually to marry and leave the family. Thus, the birth of sons was always greater cause for celebration than the birth of daughters. In modern days, of course, we can celebrate both equally intensely and observe all the good fortune rituals equally for both sons and daughters. I know I did when Jennifer was born since she was as precious to me as if I had given birth to a son.

Thus upon her birth, I gave her a long pink dress. This was because I considered the customary auspicious **red** to be a bit loud. But I did send eggs dyed red to my parents and my in laws. And I did celebrate the first month birthday with a very elaborate dinner when I invited all my friends. This celebration dinner

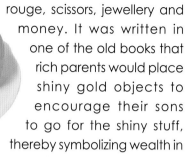

Red-dyed eggs

brings good fortune to the family since it announces a *hei see* which attracts good chi to the home. It is therefore better to hold the celebration dinner at home, since lots of people coming to the home is what brings in the yang energy. Also, the gifts of gold for the baby – bangles, bracelets and little gold coins – were symbolically most auspicious. When you are invited to a baby's month old celebration dinner therefore, do bring *a bit of gold* to present to the child. That is more meaningful than bringing toys or clothes and probably less expensive too!

In the old days, there was a ritual that was played out with baby boys to get an indication of what they would grow up to be. When a baby boy reached a hundred days old, he would be placed on a table on which would be laid out a book, a toy sword, some coins, prayer beads and a badge of office. It was then believed that whatever the baby grabbed at first would indicate the direction of his future livelihood. Baby girls could also play this game except that what was placed in front of baby girls were things like powder and

rouge, scissors, jewellery and money. It was written in one of the old books that rich parents would place shiny gold objects to encourage their sons to go for the shiny stuff, thereby symbolizing wealth in the young boy's future!

Celebrating the feast of a thousand autumns

As a general rule, it is not considered auspicious to celebrate birthdays. It is even regarded as unlucky and tempting fate to celebrate 39th, 49th and 59th birthdays since these are the ages when life obstacles could well manifest. Thus attaining these ages was often cause for worry rather than cause for celebration. The advice when we each reach these ages is to lie low, and be extra careful, because these are the ages when we can succumb to fatal illness or meet with serious accidents. It is only after one has passed the nines that one has reason to celebrate.

The Chinese generally take the attitude that birthdays, unlike marriages and births of sons were not *hei sees* (i.e. happy occasions) unless one was celebrating the great birthdays of parents. These were the sixtieth, seventieth and eightieth birthdays, which were referred to as *the feast of a thousand autumns*. This implies wishing the birthday patriarch or matriarch

longevity wishes - wishing them to live to a thousand years. Such occasions were indeed causes for celebrations and it was then maintained that the bigger these celebrations were, the greater would be the *yang* energy generated, and the greater would be the chances of living to a very old age.

Often during such occasions, the children would present auspicious longevity symbols as gifts. The most popular were the **God of Longevity** carved out of a precious material like jade or some other semi-precious stone or made of porcelain. Another extremely popular and suitable gift would be paintings of **peaches and cranes.** Sculpted in semi-precious stones, these were regarded as being extremely auspicious. These subjects were especially suitable for family patriarchs. This is because the patriarch is also symbolic of the trigram *chien*, which stands for heaven, for the deities, and for heavenly symbols. Matriarchal longevity gifts on the

other hand usually comprised landscape paintings of **bamboo** or **pine trees**, often drawn amidst clouds and water features. Matriarchs were supposed to be of the earth element as signified by the trigram *kun.* Thus earthly objects of longevity were considered more auspicious for mothers and grandmothers.

An auspicious gift for a pregnant woman

According to the Book of Odes, an old Chinese classic of customs and folklore, if you are pregnant and you dream of bears - be they black or brown or white - it indicates you will get a son. If you dream of snakes, it is an omen for the birth of a daughter. The Chinese desire for sons was for many centuries extremely unwavering. Even as recent as this century, parents in China, weighed under by the one child rule, often abandoned baby girls to allow them to try again. Thankfully, this absurd preoccupation is beginning to lose its hold.

There is a very famous painting that shows a **hundred children** playing in a garden. All the children drawn are boys and this painting is believed to be most auspicious as a gift to a pregnant woman, as it sends wishes for many sons! It is said that many masterpieces with this subject used to hang in the bedchamber of the emperors to signal the wish that the son of heaven would produce many male heirs since this was regarded as the surest way of maintaining the dynastic continuation.

Usually the best gifts for a pregnant woman would be auspicious paintings with symbolic meanings. One showing a boy mounted on a unicorn, or a boy holding a lotus signified wishes for sons. A painting of twelve children with peaches and pomegranates says *may you have a long life and plenty of children*! A painting of an old man with a child was considered auspicious since this means wishing the pregnant woman a particularly clever son. The old man here is supposed to represent the Taoist sage Lao Tze.

The aspiration of giving birth to a clever son capable of performing brilliantly at the imperial exams has been a prime aspiration of Chinese parents for over two thousand years. This was because the examinations were the best way of attaining success and high rank in the Emperor's court, a success that would benefit the entire family. It is not so different in today's world! Education is still the key to great success. So if you want to present a particularly apt gift with this auspicious meaning, I suggest you give a painting that depicts a dragon, or better yet, a dragon carp. This means a carp with the body of a fish but the head of a dragon. This implies the successful crossing of the dragon gate – the *lung men* – by the carp swimming against the current and leaping over the gate to transform into a dragon. This symbolizes the successful graduation from the exams and joining the august ranks of the officials.

Chapter Five:
Good Fortune Fruits & Flowers

Fruits and flowers are the nectar that bring auspicious energies into homes. They signify the growth energies of the wood element and the attainment of success. Fruits are the emblem of the attainment of the final goal, while flowers signify the exciting precursor to the harvest. In feng shui, there are wealth plants and prosperity fruits. There are also special good fortune flowers. **Chrysanthemums**, **Orchids**, **Hyacinths** and **Narcissus** signify an illustrious new beginning – the recognition and flowering of hidden talents. The **lotus** signify inner joy and sustenance. The **peony**, the **plum blossom** symbolize beauty, romance and purity. The **peach** symbolises longevity. The **pomegranate**

signifies descendants luck. The **lime tree** and the **orange** bring lots of gold and abundance. Enjoy the practice of feng shui by searching for all the good fortune plants available in your country. Look for the **jade plant** and **wealth creeper**.

Display plum blossoms and yellow chrysanthemums to signify a life of ease

Plum blossoms and yellow chrysanthemums are wonderful and auspicious flowers either to display, grow or present as a gift to someone. Buddhists are particularly fond of using these flowers as offerings on altars, and during the lunar New Year, these are the most auspicious flowers to display. A profusion of yellow chrysanthemums in a long vase, or a porcelain urn filled with strong blossom stalks simply convey so much powerful yang energy that it instantly attracts good luck into the home. Plum blossoms signify beauty and splendour even in winter. Thus plum blossoms and fruits symbolize beauty in adversity. It also indicates longevity, since the flowers are able to bloom on leafless and apparently lifeless branches of the tree even up to an advanced age.

Chrysanthemums signify anything that is long lasting. Thus love, success,

Chrysanthemum

commitments, luck - anything that you wish could last forever – can be augmented by displaying these beautiful autumn flowers. When combined with any of the longevity symbols like the pine or bamboo, crane or deer, the indication of longevity is considerably strengthened.

Chrysanthemums signify the ninth month of each year and indicate joy and happiness. Chrysanthemums with the plum blossom mean a life of ease from start to end.

Even in retirement you will have the good life. With nine quails, they mean nine generations living under the same roof in great harmony and peace.

Plum Blossoms

The lotus represents ultimate purity and perfection

To Buddhists all over the world, the lotus signifies the holy seat of the Lord Buddha. It is one of the eight precious objects of Buddhism. To the Chinese, the lotus symbolizes ultimate purity and perfection because it rises untainted and exquisitely beautiful from the mud. Every part of the lotus plant from its roots to its flower can be used, and each part also has deep significance and meanings. At its most esoteric, the lotus plant signifies inward *emptiness* and outward beauty and this conveys the true nature of reality according to Buddhist philosophy. Thus, images of

Buddhas are frequently shown seated on a lotus seat.

The universally popular mantra associated with Kuan Yin or the Buddha of compassion **Om Mani Padme Hum** literally means "*I pay homage to the jewel in the lotus*". In addition, the Hindu God Brahma is also illustrated seated on a lotus flower. The lotus is also a popular Taoist symbol of good fortune. It is the emblem of one of the Eight Immortals - who is seen holding a lotus pod, which some say represents descendants luck. As a symbol of auspicious *chi*, the lotus has multiple layers of good meaning which stretch from uninterrupted social advancements to examination success to great abundance. What it signifies depends on how it is represented in paintings and good fortune art.

Thus, when the lotus is depicted being held by a young man, it indicates success in relationships. A single lotus with one bud signifies perfect union. Shown with a magpie it offers examination success luck. Illustrated with a boy holding a carp, it means prosperity and abundance.

Orchids for perfection and magnolia for beauty and grace

In feng shui, almost all flowers convey beauty, grace and perfection. Flowers with thorns on their stems are not as popular as those without. Thus, the rose does not enjoy the same kind of popularity as for instance the peony as a symbol which expresses love and affection. I always advise my young readers who wish to send roses to their loved ones to make certain that the thorns have all been taken off. And since we are on the subject of roses, yellow roses are far more auspicious in terms of enhancing the relationship than red roses. Never send red roses or red flowers to anyone in the hospital as it signifies death.

Orchids signify perfection and are considered emblematic of the *superior man*. Orchids also symbolize good family luck and plenty of progeny. In any case, they are emblems of love and beauty,

Orchid

so sending orchids is a safe bet. Violet coloured orchids are said to be most auspicious.

Magnolias are symbolic of feminine beauty

Magnolia

and sweetness. It is second in popularity only to the peony for signifying a beautiful woman and marital happiness. In the old days, only emperors and members of the Imperial family were allowed to cultivate the magnolia plant. Magnolias are superb for wedding bouquets because of their symbolic meaning and because they are white in colour.

The **narcissus** is an extremely auspicious flowering bulb. Said to bestow the flowering of one's hidden talents, this flower is excellent for career people who

Narcissus

wish to have their efforts recognized and rewarded. Grow a bowl of narcissus during the lunar new year, for this is the time when the plant sends up beautiful flowers. It is also an excellent gift to wish someone plenty of career luck for the coming year.

If you cannot find narcissus, the hyacinth is a good substitute. In general, any home that has plenty of healthy flowering plants manifest good chi energy.

Place the plants that have thorns at the edge of your garden.

Grow a few varieties of good fortune flowers and organize the colours of your blooms in accordance to the five elements of your compass direction sectors.

Thus, reds and oranges for the South; white for the West and Northwest, blues and violets for the North and yellows for everywhere else.

A lime plant laden with fruit is extra auspicious in the new year

The image shown on the facing page is a lime plant laden with ripe fruit - an image of abundance placed just outside the main front door. This healthy growing plant brings money luck to any home that grows it, but is considered extra auspicious during the lunar New Year. During the fifteen days of celebrations, a lime tree placed by the two sides of the main door brings prosperity luck throughout the year.

The origins of this symbolism lie in the Chinese pre-occupation with oranges. During the time of the Ming emperors, annual tributes of oranges were sent to the Imperial capital from the southern provinces. Because of the long journey to the capital, these auspicious fruits were transported in the form of potted plants so that by the time they arrived in Beijing, the fruits had ripened and had turned an auspicious orange. In Malaysia and Singapore today, many corporate businesses deliver a pair of potted lime trees to their favoured customers and important associates during the New Year

as a gesture of appreciation for business given through the year. Local nurseries have also perfected the art of getting the plants to flower at precisely the right time, so that during the New Year, the fruits would have ripened.

The pomegranate is another popular and lucky fruit. This fruit comes in a shade of brilliant red, and it bursts open to reveal plenty of seeds. This is the reason it is regarded as a symbol of fertility. The fruit is said to create the luck for many sons.

Pomegranate

The pomegranate also symbolizes a family blessed with filial children who will each grow up to bring honour and glory to the family. Eaten during the New Year, it is said that mothers can expect to give birth to sons during the course of the year. The pomegranate plant is highly prized by Buddhists who use it in their prayer rituals.

The orange is like gold in feng shui

The orange is regarded as being a fruit that signifies gold - which in turn is another word for *extreme good fortune*. Since it is gold, the orange is considered to be extremely auspicious and is thus a *de rigeur* part of the New Year festivities. In fact, New Year is considered incomplete without the orange.

This is because the word for orange is *kum*, which is also the word for gold. There are many varieties of oranges in China. The popular variety used for the New year

Display an orange gem tree in your living room to greet in the New Year. Select one that is laden with fruits. Tie 9 'gold' coins to the tree and also tie red ribbon to energise it for the coming year.

celebrations are the brightly coloured mandarin oranges.

Other auspicious varieties are the cinnabar coloured variety, which some say is similar to the peach fruit of immortality. Such coloured oranges are believed to have been used in Taoist alchemy.

It is a good idea to lavishly display oranges in the home during the fifteen days of the Lunar New Year. This ostensibly ensures that there will be happiness and prosperity in the household throughout the coming twelve months. Oranges are

also given to relatives and friends, to wish them similar prosperity for the coming twelve months.

Those with altars can place nine oranges stuck with red paper as offerings to their Buddhas and deities. This too is considered as auspicious, since it signifies offering gold to the deities.

The peel of the orange is meanwhile regarded as having medicinal qualities. Dried orange peel are a favourite cure for all kinds of stomach ailments and also used as a sedative.

The jade plant is a great favourite with the chinese

I was told years ago that the Chinese value the jade plant highly because it signified the tree of wealth or money plant. I never laid it much credence until I started writing feng shui books and started becoming increasingly more observant and aware of my surroundings. That was when I started noticing just how many successful Chinese restaurants in London had these plants.

They placed these plants near the entrance to their restaurants where I had been told they should be placed to create success luck for the business. These plants are also good in the Southeast to energize the money luck of this corner. I first heard of the jade plant while based in Hong Kong many years ago. It was explained to me that the succulent leaves of the plant resembled jade, a precious stone highly valued by the Chinese for its many attributes. A jade plant was thus the nearest thing to the **wish fulfilling gem tree** so highly prized as a decorative object of great excellence. In recent years, many of

Wish Fulfilling Gem Tree

Money Plant

these gem trees have come out of South Africa. They are made of metal wire and come in a variety of semi precious stones including jasper, cornelian, natural crystals and amethysts.

These gem trees simulate the jade plant but of course, for those of you who can find such a plant, there is nothing like the real thing. Good substitutes to the jade plant are other species of succulent cactus plants. These even look prosperous! Their leaves are thick with water. Do not mix these up with the thorny cactus, which are not auspicious. Indeed, any plants with sharp pointed thorns are said to send out slivers of poison arrows that create bad luck. Thorny plants are best confined to the edges of the garden where they can take on the role of repelling unwanted visitors and protecting the house.

In Malaysia and Singapore, a variety of plant that is regarded as the **money** plant is the creeper plant with heart shaped leaves which can be grown both indoors or outdoors. These money plants grow very

easily in water. Their leaves are green and yellow in colour and they are best grown in the East or Southeast.

Outdoors, these plants can sometimes magnify in size and become huge creeper plants that cling onto trees as parasitic plants. Grown this way they lose their auspicious attributes.

Good fortune fruits include the lychee and the persimmon

The lychee is reputed to signify a marriage union that is blessed with clever children when it is drawn with the longan. Young married women are encouraged to eat the lychee and longan fruit to create this luck for themselves. The lychee is also regarded as a symbol of shrewdness, and is thus considered good for business people. Paintings of auspicious fruits should always include the lychee.

According to feng shui, it is considered auspicious to hang a painting of fruits in

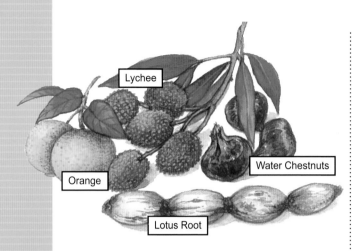

Lychee

Orange

Water Chestnuts

Lotus Root

the dining room. The illustration shown above combines four auspicious fruits - the lychee, the water chestnut, the orange and the lotus root. Each of these items indicates a special attribute of good luck. The lychee and water chestnuts denote clever children in the family; the oranges denote prosperity while the lotus root denotes the nature of life.

The persimmon is a very fortunate fruit with wonderful meaning for those in business. As a plant, the persimmon has several lucky attributes. It is said to signify longevity, kindness and astuteness. The persimmon plant is therefore found in many gardens. It also possesses other auspicious meanings, especially when displayed with other symbols of good fortune.

Thus, when placed with mandarin oranges, the combined symbolism means success in all business ventures undertaken. It is for this reason that Hong Kong restaurants knowledgeable about the symbolism of fruits often serve tangerines with persimmons as a gesture of good wishes to their corporate customer for business success at the end of a meal. In

the same way, persimmon served with the lychee fruit signifies profit being made from trading. Once again, it is an auspicious business indication.

In paintings, the persimmon fruit is also frequently drawn with other symbols of good fortune. Thus, when featured with magnolias and magic mushrooms (shown below) the meaning is once again success in business.

It is therefore extremely recommended to make gifts of persimmons to your business associates, customers and important partners.

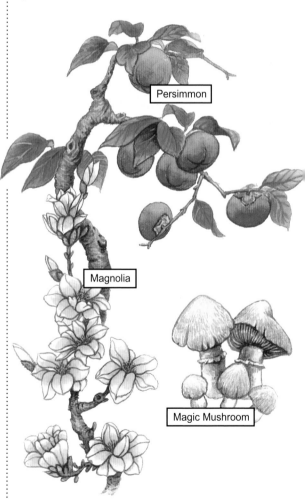

Persimmon

Magnolia

Magic Mushroom

The flowers of the four seasons for year round luck

The flowers of the four seasons represent happiness and good fortune throughout the year. It is an excellent idea to display them in the home to encourage the smooth flow of happy energy.

At the start of the year, the flowers of Spring are the iris and the magnolia. In the summer, the peony and the lotus bring good luck. In the autumn, it is the chrysanthemum that attracts good fortune. And in the winter months, it is the plum blossom. According to the Book of Odes, doorways benefit from a display of magnolias, and peonies bring good luck when placed high up.

Orchids should be hung along corridors and winter blossoms should be placed in large porcelain vases. Chrysanthemums should be displayed on altars and the lotus should be mixed with lilies in the garden.

Most auspicious of all for the young ladies of the family is a display of peonies. Use silk peonies to get them in glorious colours and to guard against them fading.

In the illustration here, peonies have been combined with the magnolia and plum blossom and displayed in a broad porcelain vase, which signifies excellent marriage luck for the daughters of the family.

There are many different lists of flowers. Thus there are the twelve flowers of the

Plum Blossoms

Magnolias

Chrysanthemums

Peonies

twelve months, which include all the blossoms, and auspicious flowers already mentioned.

The display of flowers in the home has always been considered as indicating various types of good fortune. Different flowers denote different things and in the Book of Odes, there are many descriptions of how flowers are to be displayed.

The most important criteria is to remember that flowers should never be allowed to fade while on display in the house. As soon as there are signs of wilting, it should be instantly removed, otherwise they emit harmful *yin* energy. In this connection, the use of driftwood in flower arrangements is not regarded as an auspicious arrangement.

Plant a *money tree* in your garden to get seriously rich

There is an old Chinese legend that refers to a money tree that has branches of coins and gold. When you shake the money tree, gold coins fall like rain as if from heaven into your garden. This rainfall of coins and gold has thus become a popular motif in old paintings and screens, and needless to say has become a great favourite with enthusiasts who believe in the power of symbolic feng shui. You can *grow* a money tree in your garden by using lots of old coins. Use your creativity to create such a tree paying close attention to the tying of coins to hang auspiciously down the tree as shown in the photo here.

Note that the hanging coins are tied together with red thread. Amongst the branches is a dragon and this adds further symbolism to the tree. On the stem of the tree are auspicious Chinese characters and inscriptions, and at the base of the tree are three red lanterns, which serve to energize the tree. In the picture little boys are shown sweeping coins which have fallen from the tree. This is symbolic of the *harvesting of coins*. The expression *shaking the money tree* always

means getting rich with little effort. It does not always have positive connotations!

Coins have always played a big role in Chinese belief systems. For a long time, they were used as amulets - protective devices against thieves and bad spirits. In practice these coins were worn around the neck with red thread; or tied, again with red thread to look like swords.

Coins were also used to create wealth luck and this was done by tying them into elaborate auspicious designs, in lucky numbers and with red thread.

For the wealth tree, coins should be tied into strands of a thousand coins so that the expression will be a tree with *ten thousand coins*. Most auspicious this way. During the lunar new year, red lanterns were hung from the wealth tree to signify *wealth all year round*.

A variation of the money tree is the **gem tree**, and this is made entirely of semi precious stones like crystals, amethysts, cornelian, citrines or coral. The stems are usually made of gold. These gem trees are extremely auspicious since they create wonderful lucky energy for the whole house.

I keep mine (made of cornelian) in the NW side of my living room since this is the corner of chien, thereby signifying *wealth from heaven*.

> The gem tree is most auspicious when it has a solid trunk and is tied with gold coins.

Chapter Six:
Symbols of Protection

Incorporating symbols of protection into the environment of our living and work space is a significant branch of the practice of Chinese feng shui. In China, **Door Gods** and **Fu Dogs** symbolically guard all the temples, the palaces of the Imperial family, as well as the homes of high level officials. Usually displayed as a pair, fu dogs are legendary creatures that are often mistaken for Unicorns. Some regard them as **lions**, others as a combination of several auspicious creatures. There are other protective

symbols - the Tiger, the Eagle, and in fact any fierce big animal placed by the outside entrance of any abode becomes a protector symbol.

In addition, feng shui also speaks of the potency of the **simple fan** which controls the wind in paper and of the red lanterns that control fire within paper.

Special **Taoist amulets** that protect against accidents and misfortune also feature strongly in traditional feng shui practice. Discover all the different ways to safeguard your luck and well being by cleverly using protective and defensive objects. Learn how to use cures and antidotes to feng shui problems, thereby protecting against bad luck.

The white tiger is the companion of the green dragon and also protects

The great practice of feng shui can be described as the auspicious meeting of the dragon and the tiger - the two great forces of the Universe that reflect the primordial yin and yang of existence. To the Chinese, the tiger is the emblem of dignity, sternness, courage and ferocity. It is yin where the dragon is yang.

The white tiger brings great good fortune when paired with the celestial dragon and it also protects. It signifies the compass direction of the West and in terms of orientation, the intangible spirit of the tiger is said to be on the right hand side of the main door. (i.e. standing at the door and looking outwards). Usually, it is not advisable to place the image of the tiger inside the home, as there is the danger that this creature can turn its ferocity against the house. Unless residents are born in animal years of the tiger or dragon, this danger becomes very real. In a tiger year, the tiger presence in the house in the form of paintings or sculptures can be dangerous omens of accidents and illness.

The tiger is best regarded as a symbol of protection and for this, it is good to place his image outside the house by the side of the main door. This ensures that people with bad intentions, towards the resident family and its members, do not gain entry.

One of the best symbols of protection is said to be a picture of three white tigers, and this should be hung outside the house near the vicinity of the front door. In Taoist temples, doors are frequently drawn with the image of the white tiger.

In certain parts of China and Asia, the tiger is regarded as the God of Wealth, and it is probably not a coincidence that the most popular God of wealth known as **Tsai Shen Yeh** is frequently depicted sitting on a tiger. A picture of this deity of wealth is shown here. Note the dragon image on the front of the robes worn by the God of wealth and note that he sits on a tiger. This symbolizes the supremacy of the intangible forces of the dragon resulting in the successful harnessing in turn of the tiger's intangible spirit. If you display this image in your home, your family will be strongly protected from poverty and during good times, he brings great prosperity.

A pair of lions offers sacred protection

The lion is not indigenous to China and it is speculated that its image came with the rise in influence of Buddhism. This is because the snow lion is sacred to Buddhism and is often shown offering flowers to Buddha. The lion is regarded as an emblem of courage, boldness and bravery. It is a valiant creature who possesses prudence and sagacity.

The Buddha Manjushuri is sometimes depicted seated astride a lion, his right hand wielding the sword of wisdom. In the old days, top military officials of the second grade had lion images embroidered onto their court robes.

Snow Lion guarding the Potala Palace in Tibet

A pair of Fu Dogs (from outside looking in), with the female on the left and the male on the right.

The lion is also said to be an excellent guardian protector of buildings, particularly sacred buildings - hence the frequency of its usage as temple protectors. Large sculpted stone lions are placed flanking main doors, usually one on either side of the door. They are also situated along entrance corridors and guarding the porticos of homes. Sometimes they can also be seen guarding the tombs of ancestral graves. In appearance, the protective Chinese lions look formidable. He is drawn with big eyes and a fierce countenance, but it is not generally regarded as a formidable beast. The lion is not as greatly feared as the tiger. The Chinese lion also bears little resemblance to the African lions that we know of today. They look more like the other great protector creature, the home grown Fu Dogs. But it is easy to tell them apart. Chinese lions are almost always sculpted as a pair, as shown in the picture. The male has his foot resting on a globe while the female carries her child. For protection against bad intangible forces, place a pair of lions (get smaller sized varieties done in glazed ceramics) flanking your main door outside. Place the male on the left and the female on the right (inside looking out).

A pair of Fu Dogs on either side of your front entrance is believed to ward off killing energy and prevents people with evil intentions from entering your house.

Fu dogs afford symbolic protection against killing chi

Feng shui Masters freely recommend the placement of a pair of fu dogs at the front entrance door. This is believed to ward off killing energy and prevent people with evil intentions from entering the house. In appearance, fu dogs look remarkably similar to lions, but there are subtle differences. Fu dogs are mythical creatures frequently shown playing with a ball, which may be the sun, the yin yang egg symbol or simply a precious stone or a pearl. This is usually left to one's imagination. It is the male fu dog that plays with the ball. Sometimes two fu dogs are shown playing and frolicking and this representation is often compared to two dragons playing with the pearl. There are many different images and representations of Fu Dogs inside the palace compounds of the Forbidden City in Beijing. Fu Dogs were deemed excellent protectors for palaces, and homes of the emperors, as opposed to lions being more suitable for religious

places of meditation and worship. Fu Dogs are thus the more suitable of the two for residential homes.

Choose ceramic fu dogs that differentiate between the male and the female, and always place them with the male (the one with the ball) on the left hand side of the door and the female on the other side. It is not necessary to get them too large, but it is a good idea to place them fairly high up. I put mine high up above the gate facing each other. All postures are suitable as feng shui protector images. They can be made of any material although I personally prefer them to be made of ceramic because these signify earth, since feng shui is about harnessing good earth energy.

Reviving the old tradition of placing Door Gods for protection

Once when I was very young, I accompanied my grandmother to the temple and saw colourful and fierce looking Door Gods dressed in what looked like ancient Chinese clothes.

My grandmother explained they were meant to keep out bad spirits and to make sure no *ghosts* could enter. As a result of that innocent explanation, I lived my childhood in abject fear of ghosts. Years later, when I moved to Hong Kong, I came across antique doors with pictures of these protective deities and true to form, I succumbed to the nostalgia of my grandmother's story and bought them on the spot. For a time, they guarded my home in Hong Kong until I moved back to Malaysia.

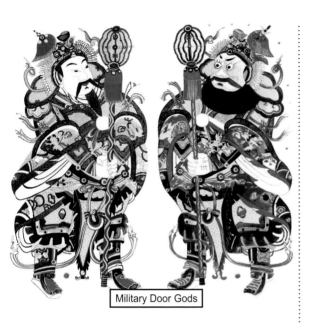

Military Door Gods

Civilian Door God

Military Door Gods originated in the Tang Dynasty. They are based on two loyal generals *Chin* and *Yu* who stood guard over the emperor's quarters through the night to ensure the son of heaven would sleep peacefully and not be disturbed by either spirits or ghosts. They themselves however soon succumbed to their nocturnal duties so the emperor hit on the idea of painting their images onto entrance doors into his private quarters. Court painters were commissioned to draw two pictures of fully armed generals wearing armour and carrying weapons. The Generals eventually came to be known as military Door Gods and with the passage of time, they were drawn one with a white face and one with a black face. The practice became popular and continued to be observed well into the present century.

A less frightening version are the **Civilian Door Gods** who look less threatening. These Gods are also to be displayed in a pair but they can be drawn in court robes giving them the appearance of courtiers rather than fighters. Their protective powers are deemed symbolic rather than actual and they guard against bad luck rather than ghosts and spirits. Those who want to revive this old custom of painting door Gods on their homes might want to consider these civilian Gods rather than the military version. Also, the advice from a feng shui master is that if you do have these Gods painted on your front doors, make sure the doors themselves are painted red.

Kuan Kung is the patron deity of police & triads alike

Of the many colourful deities of the Chinese pantheon, there is probably none as popular or colourful as the God of War **Kuan Kung** also known as Kuan Ti who is regarded as a God of Wealth. He is, amongst many other titles, the protector of the oppressed, patron saint of police, guardian deity of the triads, and in recent times, protector of politicians and business leaders alike. Images of Kuan Kung sell like hot cakes. Whether standing or sitting, on horseback or glaring at his enemies, Kuan Kung in your house brings with it his powerful energy. Place Kuan Kung high up watching the front door! The more fierce his countenance, the more

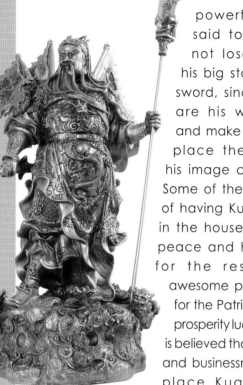

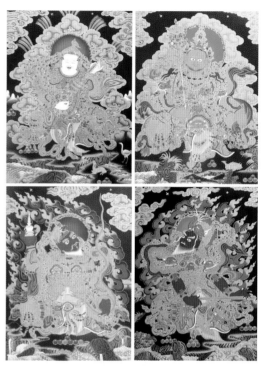

powerful he is said to be. Do not lose either his big staff or his sword, since these are his weapons and make sure you place them onto his image correctly. Some of the benefits of having Kuan Kung in the house include peace and harmony for the residents, awesome protection for the Patriarch and prosperity luck for all. It is believed that leaders and businessmen who place Kuan Kung behind them at work will never lack for powerful support from important people.

Kuan Kung is most powerful when placed in the NW corner of a house. He should always face the main door, so that he has his eye on who comes in and out of the house. There is no necessity to worship Kuan Kung. From a feng shui perspective, his image is all you need. I have several Kuan Kungs in my house, and continue to be fascinated by the symbolic power of this red faced general who lived during the times of the warring states.

Those wishing to familiarize themselves with the story of Kuan Kung can read *Romance of the Three Kingdoms*, a popular classic literature of intrigues that reflect the political and military environment of those times.

Four Heavenly Kings guard the four directions

The Four Heavenly Kings have fascinated me ever since I can remember. They are known also as Dharma Protectors by Mahayana Buddhists, and as Deva Kings in Sanskrit by the Hindus. These four celestial beings are fabled to be the guardians of the slopes of Mount Meru, a Buddhist paradise. From there, they supposedly protect the Universe against attacks by evil forces and spirits of the four directions. Buddhist meditation centers and temples in China have life-sized images at their entrances, placed two on each side. In Tibetan *thangka* paintings of Buddhist deities, the Heavenly Kings are usually drawn as Dharma Protectors.

The four heavenly kings are usually depicted as heavily armed, each holding a personalized weapon each with vast supernatural powers. They are always

Getting to know the four heavenly kings ...

The Guardian of the East is *Mo Li Ching*. Also known as Chiguk, and as the great king Dhritarashtra in the language of Sanskrit (as referred to in the great Suvarnabhasa the Golden light sutra) this king has a white face, a fierce expression and a beard that looks like copper wire. He carries a four-string mandolin or pi-pa, which when strummed causes great balls of the fire to drop from the sky onto those who would dare to invade his space. His weapon is associated with the fire element, which can easily subdue the wood element of the East. In this way, he keeps firm control over his domain. He is the most senior of the four kings. The name of this figure means "the Heavenly King who protects the nation." From the Eastern slope of Sumeru Mountain, he keeps the kingdom safe and eases the life of the ordinary people. In textual accounts his weapons vary, but most often he is drawn carrying a lute. By playing this instrument, he is able to control the weather. Place him in the East or looking at the main door, alert to whatever evil forces may seek to enter the home.

The Guardian of the West is *Mo Li Hai*. Also known as Kwangmol, and as the great king Virupaksa in the language of Sanskrit (as referred to in the great Suvarnabhasa the Golden light sutra) this king has a dark maroon face and carries a pearl in one hand and a snake in the other. The full name of the Western Heavenly King means "evil eye." His common name, however, means "broad eye" or wide-seeing one. In the Kwangmok aspect, this kings holds a writhing dragon in one hand and a jewel in the other. The jewel symbolizes the world, and the western king prevents its theft. If you place an image of this heavenly kings facing the main door, your home will be protected from evil influences. The heavenly kings also ensure that residents do not engage in activities that causes the accumulation of negative karma.

The Guardian of the South is *Mo Li Hung*. Also known as Chungchang, and as the great king Virudhaka in the language of Sanskrit (as referred to in the great Suvarnabhasa the Golden light sutra) this king has a blue face. He carries a spear and a precious magical sword that has the characters earth, water, fire and wind etched onto its blade. His sword has the power to create a black wind, which produces a million spears that pierced through the bodies of evil nagas reducing them to dust. The wind is then followed by fire, which fills the space with a million serpents. The expression on his face is always fierce and piercing. Place his image alongside the other kings facing the front of the home.

The Guardian of the North is *Mo Li Shou*. Also known as Tamun, and as the great king Vaisravana, he has a black face and carries a magic umbrella whose supernatural powers protects against thunderstorms. Anytime the umbrella is opened, it creates total darkness. When the umbrella is reversed, it creates huge earthquakes and gigantic tidal waves that have the power to completely destroy negative forces originating from the North. This king's name means "repeatedly-expanding or growing King." The umbrella he carries will multiply according to the number of his enemies. Mo Li Shou has heard more of Buddha's teachings than anyone else, so he is sometimes shown holding a stupa, the base of which represents earth and the roof represents heaven.

Buddhist regard Vaisravana as the Guardian protector of one's wealth, and thangkas of this king are often mistaken for the Yellow Jhambala or Wealth Buddha. He is said to have practiced austerity for a thousand years and has thus been rewarded with great wealth. He is also called Kuvera, the "God of Wealth." In his palace in the Himalayas, he is attended by Yaksas (guardians of the earth's treasures) and Kinnaras (celestial musicians similar to Greek centaurs). Statues sometimes show him with a sword, a trident, or a banner (representing his triumphs) in his right hand. His body is sometimes painted yellow, signifying it is as bright as a thousand suns. In his left hand, a jewel-spitting mongoose provides sentient beings with inexhaustible wealth. Of the four heavenly kings, he is the one regarded as the most popular, probably because he is associated with the Wealth Buddha.

shown alert and ready to ward off negative influences, and they are said to be powerful protectors for those requiring protection from evil demons and spirits. With them in your home, it is believed that righteousness, honesty and good moral character will prevail. They defend with tireless energy and their power is said to be invincible.

These *kings* can be considered to be holy images of celestial beings of the Buddhist pantheon of deities, and as such they may not be suitable for those of my readers of other faiths. In this connection, I should explain that the practice of symbolic feng shui to create an environment of harmony and peace in the home borrows much from symbols that are both esoteric and spiritual. In instances, these symbols often reflect the three main religious philosophies of China - Taoism, Buddhism and Confucianism.

The four heavenly kings are well known Guardian Deities and are used as such in Chinese homes and temples to complement other feng shui features. But readers should exercise their own discretion on the use of these particular symbols.

Do not place the heavenly kings outside the home. Place them inside the home, preferably on either side of your altar. Or, if you have a holy *stupa* inside the house, you can also place them one on each corner facing the four cardinal directions. This takes care of evil influences and temptations that come from the four directions. It is important to place the correct heavenly king properly. They should either face the direction or be situated in the location that corresponds to their individual domains. This is because each of the kings is said to have his own domain.

Taoist amulets for physical safety

In addition to bringing good luck, feng shui is also supposed to offer protection against bad luck that can come in different guises. An interesting branch of feng shui involves harnessing all the methods used in the past to ward off negative *chi* that bring accidents, illness, robbery and physical discomforts. In the old days, the use of Taoist amulets was both widespread and popular. Thus different types of talismans are referred to in the oldest Chinese texts.

Various materials were used in the fashioning of these talismans although rice paper that was coloured yellow or green were extremely popular. On these pieces of paper would be written special characters deemed to have the power to keep bad luck at bay. Illustrated here is an example of a Taoist amulet drawn with the celestial kings of the four directions. These talismans

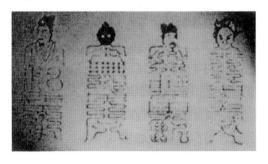

were credited with the power of dissolving *bad chi* caused by wandering bad spirits. Different characters could also be written for different purposes. Thus there were special protection amulets for pregnant women; for protection against accidents, against fire, against water and so forth. The amulet shown here is an example of one worn by pregnant women to protect the unborn child from coming to any harm.

Handwritten amulets were believed to be especially powerful for warding off physical harm. They gave protection from being assaulted and even against armed robberies. There are feng shui masters who are particularly adept at writing these protective amulets. Special characters are drawn on green paper after chanting some Taoist prayers. I have carried protective amulets for over twenty years and have found them really potent for warding off physical harm.

Amulets should never be sold on a commercial basis. Those of you fortunate enough to know high temple lamas or holy men can request for protection amulets. To get one, all you have to do is ask, or you can purchase a protective symbol and then ask a high priest or temple abbot to bless them.

From the chinese almanac comes different charms for different purposes

The Chinese Almanac or **Tung Shu** contains some of the more common amulets that continue to be used these days. Those of you who wish may want to copy these charms onto yellow or green rice paper.

The charm shown here is a general house protection amulet which guards against negative influences caused by people with bad intentions towards you. It is also believed to be a good amulet against being robbed. Copy it onto yellow or dark green paper and paste it directly above your front door for protection. Paste it outside the house, facing outwards. This amulet is also believed to be effective against *spells* being cast onto members of the household.

This next charm, shown here, also written on paper is effective for curing fever and other types of ailments. According to the Chinese Almanac, you should copy this charm onto a piece of yellow rice paper, burn it and then place the ashes in water and drink the water.

This will bring the fever down quickly. This charm on the right can also be placed inside a metal container and worn around the neck to protect you against epidemics and other outbreaks of diseases.

The charm shown on the right here is effective against any bad chi or bad spirit you feel may be *haunting* your house.

Copy and fix it to the part of the house where you are getting strange vibes.

The charm on the far right is effective for eye ailments and abdominal pains. Burn it and put the ashes in water then use the water to bathe your eyes or drink it if you have abdominal pains.

From *tibetan feng shui* comes this powerful illustrated amulet

One of the most exciting discoveries I made was the existence of a book written in Tibetan entitled *"Warding Off Bad Luck from the Ten Directions"*. It was my Buddhist lama who told me about the existence of this book. My first reaction was that there are basically eight main directions, not ten; to which my lama replied, "*the other two directions are bad luck from below and bad luck from above*". Of course my lama was right and I am hoping one day that he will kindly translate the rest of this powerful text so that the secrets of the Tibetan masters can be shared with the world.

In the meanwhile, all I have to share with you is this absolutely powerful

I reproduce my copy here for those who might be interested in copying it and hanging it inside their house for protection.

illustrated symbol of protection, which come from Tibetan sources. It shows the stomach of the tortoise and has many other symbols as well, including the trigrams and the 12 animals.

Dragons & coins can be used as feng shui talismans

The use of protective talismans is part of the cultural backdrop against which feng shui practice can be studied and understood. On the one hand, wearing talismans can be regarded as superstition. On the other hand, because they are so much a part of the traditional protective mentality of the Chinese, they seem to neatly complement the practice of feng shui, and indeed even be regarded as an adjunct of symbolic

feng shui. Another important observation I made throughout my years of investigation into feng shui is the fact that almost all the authentic practising masters of feng shui had at least some knowledge of amulets and talismans.

All seemed familiar with using some form of protection. Many went to great pains to explain to me that feng shui consultants often encountered hazards in the course of their work, so carrying symbolic protection was something all feng shui practitioners knew about. Sometimes it is possible that negative spirits and influences haunted homes they go to feng shui, and amulets are believed to protect them from succumbing to illness or other more severe afflictions caused by the *dirty energy* of such homes. It is for this reason also that many feng shui masters are armed with many different types of powerful talismans usually given to them by their teachers.

Dragon amulets such as the ones illustrated here can be extremely powerful for protecting against being harmed by what is termed *dirty energy* left over in houses that have had a history of afflicted or bad feng shui.

Traditional coin amulets were worn around the neck.

The *Lo Shu* and Dragon Tortoise protect against wrong orientations

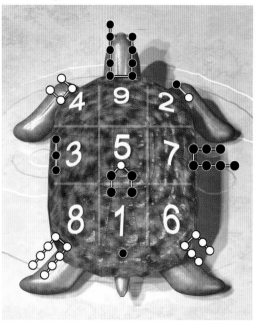

In attempting to unlock the secrets of the eight trigrams that are placed around the Pa Kua, ancient and latter day feng shui scholars focused on the mysterious **Lo Shu** and **Ho Tu** grids. Of the two, it is the **Lo Shu** which is better known and which has come to be called the *magic square*. The numbers of the Lo Shu are arranged in such a way that adding them in any direction along any three points in a straight line (whether horizontally, vertically or diagonally) add up to the number 15. This coincides to the number of days in each of the 24 phases of the solar year or how long it takes a new moon to become a full moon. In other words, the

Lo Shu expresses one cycle of the waxing and waning moon. Look at the numbers in the square on the back of the tortoise and you will see how the numbers add up to 15. The story of the Lo Shu is that a tortoise with a dragon's head referred to as the **noble tortoise** emerged from the legendary river Lo carrying these huge numbers on its back arranged in a grid pattern as shown. These numbers appeared in the form of dots that added up to a certain number. The story goes that the legendary emperor *Fu Hsi* deciphered these numbers on the tortoise's back and successfully used them to unlock the secrets of the Pa Kua and its eight trigrams. The result spawned the practice of feng shui that is based on the Lo Shu square. The Lo Shu is regarded as a magic square. Displaying it in conjunction with the noble dragon tortoise is said to attract good feng shui. But together they also have the capability of warding off bad forces that get created for individual residents due to harmful orientations that are based on dates of birth and gender.

Those of you familiar with my book *"Eight Mansions Feng Shui"* will know of this particular compass formula which has proved to be so potent when applied correctly. If you happen to live in a house where the orientations of the main door and rooms are not auspicious for you, and you have no choice, try displaying a dragon tortoise and a Lo Shu square. This should offer protection from any bad feng shui resulting from unfortunate orientations.

The *Ho Tu* grid and Dragon Horse can defeat bad *flying stars*

Like the Lo Shu square, the *ho tu* grid of numbers is also said to have protective capabilities that can overcome the effect of bad *flying stars*. For those of you unfamiliar with flying star feng shui, this is a divinitive school of feng shui which spells out the technique of casting the natal charts of houses based on when they were built or last renovated. This formula tracks the *time dimension* feng shui of homes and can predict when bad or good things can happen depending on where the main door and bedrooms are located. This is based on the premise that every sector of the house has periods of good or bad feng shui and these periods can be defined as days, weeks, months, years or periods of twenty years. The *stars* referred to here are good and bad numbers that move (or fly) from one compass sector of the house to another, thereby bringing good luck and bad luck at different times.

Mastering flying star can be time consuming. It is one of the more complex of feng shui formulas, so those who may not have the inclination to investigate the flying stars of their homes can use this particular recommendation which is much easier. The tip is to overcome the feng shui of bad stars by displaying the two symbols shown.

Those familiar with Flying Star feng shui may wonder why I am recommending the use of the *ho tu* and not the *lo shu*, since the flying star grid is in fact based on the *lo shu* square. This is because for the more advanced interpretations of flying star periods, it is the *ho tu* chart that

Dragon Horse with Ho Tu grid

determines good and bad dates. So the *ho tu* is believed to be the key that determines the good and bad dates for individuals.

Copy the *ho tu* numbers arranged as above and place it next to the dragon horse - then display both in the living room near the vicinity of the main door but not directly facing the door. A good place to have it is diagonal to the main door with the horse seeming to look at the door.

Use the Pa Kua Mirror to overcome all *external* poison arrows

The Pa Kua Mirror is probably the most well known of all the feng shui symbols of protection, but it is also one that has been the most incorrectly used. This eight-sided shape drawn with the eight trigrams allocated around the eight sides according to the Earlier Heaven Arrangement has a mirror in the center.

The pa kua on the left has a flat mirror in the center while the pa kua on the right has a convex mirror which protrudes outwards.

This mirror is believed to reflect back whatever bad vibes or energy is coming against your house. Thus, if a sharp or pointed or hostile structure is directly facing your main door, then placing the **pa kua mirror** directly above your door facing the structure will send all bad energy back to where it came from, thereby protecting the door and the house.

But it must be hung outside the home. Because of the way the Pa Kua works, it must face out. It must never face in. It should also never be hung anywhere inside the house, since it sends out powerful killing energy of its own that will hurt residents who confront or face it directly.

The mirror that is placed in the center of the Pa Kua can be convex, concave or flat. Pa Kuas with convex mirrors protrude outwards and these mirrors reflect and send back the negative energy. It is the most harmful of the three types of mirrors and one I recommend the least of all.

Pa Kuas with concave mirrors are depressed inwards and they absorb and draw in all the bad energy into themselves.

This is the least harmful of the three types of mirrors and the one I recommend the most, since it corrects the bad feng shui without sending out too much negative energy of its own. Pa Kuas with flat mirrors are the most common and these neither absorb nor double any bad energy being reflected back.

Carry small hand mirrors to protect against other people's bad intentions

An old tale from my great grandmother's day explains that mirrors make spirits visible. For many years, my mother carried a mirror given to her by my great grandmother - a mirror she insists protects her from being charmed and from being cheated by "bad" people. It is a very small hand mirror made of silver with very pretty engravings.

She gave it to me when I graduated from University and I used it as a makeup mirror for many years. Then last year when I went on a pilgrimage to the *Solu Khumbu* region of the Himalayas, I parted with my mirror. I was visiting the stupa that contained the relics of the holy lama of that region - a lama who has reincarnated and is now my holy lama in this life. Something made me place the mirror there at the Stupa as a kind of offering, because I did not have anything else that was suitable on me. It was a totally spontaneous action, since I knew that giving mirrors to someone means good luck.

So I believed it made a suitable and respectful *offering*. But I felt the lack of my personal mirror since and searched for a long time to find something similar. Last year I found it and I had it reproduce.

There are many superstitious beliefs associated with mirrors. It is said that if you look into your mirror and cannot recognize yourself, it means you will soon succumb to an illness. It is bad luck to have mirrors in the bedroom directly reflecting the bed. It is bad luck to dream of mirrors in the night but very fortunate when you dream of a mirror reflecting the sun or sunlight.

If you receive a mirror as a gift, it means you will soon get married, have a son or get a promotion. In any case, it means good luck. If you give a mirror as a gift to a career person, it means they will soon enjoy a quantum and unexpected leap into high office.

Decorative mirrors made of bronze, silver or gold have been used in China and carried by the women of high families ever since the second millennium BC. There are many stories of how these mirrors were actually magic mirrors capable of protecting the women from harm.

Mirrors also feature strongly in Buddhist rituals used by high lamas and monks in their purification ceremonies and prayer sessions. The best *magic mirrors* were said to be those that were made on auspicious days from special sand taken from central China.

A sandalwood fan is an excellent deflector of bad energy

When I first started lecturing on feng shui around the world, I used to carry a sandalwood fan with me as this is supposed to ward off bad energy that inadvertently gets sent one's way. Several of my my feng shui *sifus* told me to carry a fan since this would simulate a screening effect that would deflect any negative energy. They explained that fans were supposed to have the power to deflect hostile chi. The Chinese regard the fan as *wind in paper* since it is mostly made of paper stuck on sandal wood. But fans also come in tortoise shell since this is supposed to enhance its esoteric powers of protection.

Fans have been used since ancient times. There are many variations and they come in a variety of shapes, although the round shape is popular. The folding variety is a Japanese invention introduced into China in the 11th century through Korea.

Irrespective of their shapes, the fan is a popular accessory carried by both men and women alike. Men carried fans in their sleeves or waistband. They often brought out their fans while discussing matters of the court, as much to emphasize their viewpoint as to create an invisible *shield* that would serve to protect them against people with dishonourable or bad intentions towards them. In the atmosphere of court intrigues, fans were considered an important and significant tool.

Taoist masters often painted amulets onto specially created

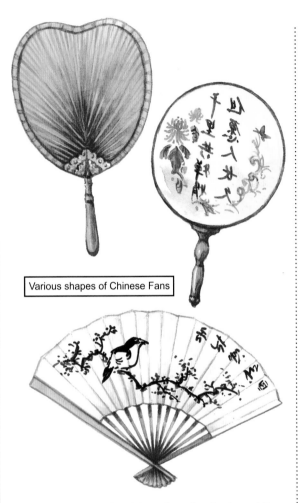

Various shapes of Chinese Fans

and personalized fans for dignitaries of the Court. Shown above are various shapes of Chinese fans. Round fans often had calligraphy and auspicious symbols painted onto them. The handles were usually also embellished with special engravings.

Scented fans, and especially sandalwood fans, are a great favourite with women, because of the special attributes of sandalwood. It is not difficult to find very intricately cut out designs on sandalwood fans in China Arts and Crafts stores in Hong Kong and China. These are usually fashioned into folding fans that can be conveniently carried in a lady's handbag.

The best antidote for the 5 yellow is the 6 rod windchime

One of the things which every feng shui practitioner must be wary of is the place of the 5 yellow each year. This is part of Flying Star feng shui. It is a major warning that is taken very seriously. The **5 yellow** is located in different sectors during different years. Suitable precautions are usually recommended to make sure one does not get hurt by the 5 yellow. The best cure for the 5 Yellow affliction is the 6-rod All-metal windchime.

Expert practitioners of flying star also recommend overcoming the influence and effect of the 5 Yellow by displaying a large painting of Zhong Kui - the most famous of Chinese heroes for overcoming black magic spells. He is also considered an exorcist of the highest ability as he is said to have 84,000 demon spirits under his command. The best time to invite him into the home (i.e. hang up his picture) is the 5th day of the 5th month. He is best placed near the front door so he can see everyone coming into the home.

Or if you wish, you can be like me and place him on the wall at the foot of the stairs. This way he protects all our upstairs bedrooms from being affected by the 5 yellow and by spirits.

Zhong Kui is frequently depicted as being exceptionally ugly with a black face. He is sometimes shown surrounded by urns of wine as he is said to be almost always

Zhong Kui

drunk. The story of his life and how he came to be what he became is a popular Chinese folk tale.

Purify your home regularly with incense blocks and singing bowls

One of the best methods of ensuring continuous good feng shui for your home is to undertake regular space cleansing and purification rituals in your home. The best and easiest way of doing this is to use incense or aroma sticks.

I use powdered sandalwood incense blocks which are locally available. The Malay name is *kemenyem* and they can be bought from almost any shop selling joss sticks and praying accessories.

I burn sandalwood incense blocks that resemble gold ingots on a special incense container. Sometimes I also sprinkle special Himalayan mountain top incense to obtain the pure energy of the Himalayas (these are very hard to get and also very expensive).

I go into every room of my home and walk round each room going clockwise; and as I do this, I let the incense clean out and purify dark corners where *bad chi* might have inadvertently been accumulating.

I allow the smoke from the incense to purify the space. I do this once a month and whenever there has been a particularly loud quarrel between residents. This cleans out all the anger energy and restores harmony once again. I also chant my favourite mantras as I move from room to room with my incense.

I have been told by my friend Denise Linn (a famous and wonderful practitioner of space cleansing as taught by the American Indians) that this is similar to the American Indian practice of scrounging homes with smoke made from burning pine branches.

7 Metal Singing Bowl

Of course pine branches always gives off a marvelous herbal type scent which must be so wonderful for making the energies crisp and clean once more. Another excellent article I discovered is the singing bowl. This beautiful object creates the most sensational sound vibrations that systematically cleanses the energies of the living space.

You can actually feel the energy of the home getting lighter and happier. For them to work however, they have to be made from seven types of metals which have to include gold and silver.

The actual mix of the metals is a closely guarded secret, but I was really lucky in that I found an old time manufacturer from Katmandu to make these bowls for me.

These singings bowls are available in two sizes and in various designs in World Of Feng Shui boutiques or *www.FSmegamall. com.*

Learn to make your bowls sing to purify the energies of your home

If you have access to getting your own singing bowls, I strongly recommend you to do so, since these bowls can be used to create sensationally crisp energy in your home. I have a hundred of these little bowls and of course I also have a huge crystal singing bowl.

When I first started using singing bowls to purify my space, the sounds came out rough and flat, but over time, as I used the bowls more and more, the sounds have been getting purer and purer. This has also coincided with the feeling of harmony amongst family members getting stronger as well.

To bring out the sounds of the singing bowl, use a wooden mallet. Get one that is made of soft wood. It is also a good idea to let the bowl sit on a small cloth cushion since this improves the sound considerably.

There are two ways to get the bowl to sing. The first is to strike the bowl firmly with the mallet. Practice several times until you get a sound that is long and sustaining, then walk round the rooms in a clockwise direction and as you strike the bowl feel the sound vibrations getting purer and purer.

The second way is a little difficult at the beginning. But it is the method of getting a more refined version of the singing sound. Use the wooden mallet and press it against the outside rim of the bowl.

Then firmly (but without exerting too much pressure) rub the bowl in a clockwise direction (i.e. moving towards you.) At first you will hear nothing, but as you learn how to vary your pressure the bowl will soon start to sing. Once you learn to make the bowl sing, use this method to create the humming sound that will cleanse all the energy in your space.

If you find it hard to find a singing bowl, you can use a metal bell as a substitute. Try to make the bell sing, using a wooden mallet in the same way and use the sound to purify the energies of your home.

Remember that the secret is to use pressure but never too much!

Chapter Seven:
The Eight Auspicious Objects

These are the eight auspicious objects in the Buddhist pantheon. These symbols of good fortune have their origins in India and Tibet, but were enthusiastically embraced by superstitious Chinese who have incorporated them into their practice of feng shui. The first of the eight auspicious objects is the Mystic Knot which signifies the state of samsara - a continuous never-ending rebirth of mankind. The knot also signifies continuing good fortune when one has succeeded in gaining good fortune, ie protection of wealth and success already attained. Then there is the Conch, which signifies good travel and communications luck. The Canopy is a powerful symbol of protection, while the Vase contains the nectar of bliss and happiness. The Wheel represents the good fortune of real wisdom and scholarship, while the Double Fish signifies material wealth. The Lotus signifies purity, and the Jar symbolizes the accumulation of family wealth.

The Mystic Knot

The mystic knot is also referred to as the endless knot and is said to "swallow its own tail". The more esoteric meaning of this symbol implies there is no beginning and no end, reflecting the Buddhist philosophy that existence is one endless round of birth and rebirth, a state the Buddhists refer to as *samsara*. The knot is thus a wonderful reminder that once we realize this great noble truth about existence, we will search for methods to be freed of this endless cycle of births and rebirths - this *samsara*.

This is what is called freedom, the freedom from samsara and from the cycle of rebirths. Buddhists of all traditions seek to attain this freedom.

This sign is also seen on the breast of the Hindu Deity Vishnu, and it is also one of the eight signs on the sole of Buddha's feet.

At a less spiritual level, the mystic knot can be seen as a symbol of a single lifetime for which it signifies a long life uninterrupted by illnesses, setbacks or sufferings.

One motif representation of the endless knot

From this viewpoint, it is also known as the *lucky knot*. In view of this, it is a very popular ornamental symbol used in a variety of ways, carved onto furniture, woven into carpets, embroidered on garments, and painted on screens and porcelain ware.

Its significance in feng shui is as an easy-to-use motif that can be incorporated into the design and pattern of grills, doors and furniture.

It is an excellent symbol of longevity and good health. Some also see it as a perfect emblem for undying love, thus it has also been identified as a lucky love symbol suitable for ensuring that the romance in a marriage will last.

It is therefore an excellent motif that can be carved on beds and furniture. This pattern can also be incorporated onto window grid designs.

The Conch or Cowrie shell for travel luck

The Conch or Cowrie shell is a symbol of a prosperous voyage. It signifies great travel luck and is particularly suitable for those who undertake a great deal of business travel. The shell is also an insignia of royalty or of royal patronage. Those engaged in the service of serving royalty would benefit from having the shell symbol worked into their house décor.

The shell is also one of the eight Buddhist auspicious objects, since it represents the voice of Buddha. It also signifies the spread

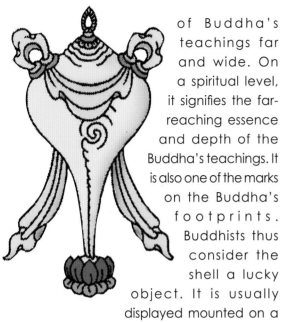

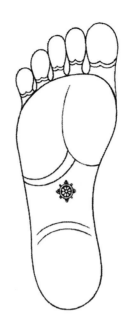

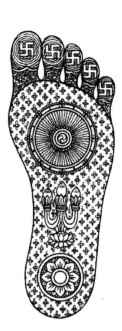

of Buddha's teachings far and wide. On a spiritual level, it signifies the far-reaching essence and depth of the Buddha's teachings. It is also one of the marks on the Buddha's footprints. Buddhists thus consider the shell a lucky object. It is usually displayed mounted on a rose wood stand, often gilded with gold or silver. Many Buddhists also purchase wonderful marine specimens of shells that they place as offerings on their altar. From a feng shui perspective, the shell can be used to attract business luck from overseas. Those engaged in export trade or whose companies depend on foreign turnover to prosper can consider displaying beautiful cowrie shells, which can be purchased from Central Market in Kuala Lumpur. These wonderful specimens collected off the tropical islands of Malaysia are inexpensive and also very suitable as feng shui energizers.

The shell is also an excellent symbol for those engaged in work, business or enterprises that benefit from them being well known, famous and respected. To create the luck of fame and reputation, place a fairly large marine specimen (about 6 to 8 inches) in the South corner of the living room. The cowrie shell can also be placed in the Northeast and Southwest to strengthen the energy of these corners. Strong energy in the NE creates excellent education luck, while strong energy in the SW enhances and improves relationship luck.

The Double Fish for wealth and protection

I have already described the wonderful symbolism of the fish - that it represents abundance, wealth, harmony and connubial bliss. When shown as a pair, the fish symbol does not merely signify happiness doubled. It also denotes the joys of physical union between lovers and spouses.

From the Buddhist perspective, the double fish symbol may be viewed as something of an amulet, which when worn as a pendant or kept as an article kept in

the wallet is a powerful charm capable of averting evil, accidents, succumbing to epidemics and bad intentions. In Thailand, a Buddhist country, the double fish symbol is elaborately fashioned in 24 carat gold and worn by children from rich families for protection. Very often, these fish amulets have been blessed by holy monks and strengthened with additional amulets

Display the auspicious Double Carp anywhere in your home to enjoy abundant good fortune. For more money, place in your wealth corner to attract prosperity luck.

written on gold foil and kept in the belly of the fish symbols. The fish is also observed to move easily in any direction in the water. An esoteric explanation of the significance of the fish symbol in Buddhism is that it signifies those who seek to attain perfect understanding of Buddha's teachings are compared to the free movement of fish where there are no obstacles and no obstructions no matter which direction is taken.

One of the most wonderful Buddhist practices said to generate enormous karmic merit is the liberation of living creatures, and liberating the fish brings good luck. Thus when you purchase fish that was meant to be eaten and then release it, it is a very good deed. If you cannot do this, you can perhaps consider stopping the practice of eating live fish in the restaurant, i.e. fresh fish that is still alive and swimming.

Having a fish killed specially for you to eat is the antithesis of fish liberation. If you eat fish that has already been killed, you are said to be eating a carcass and there is no negative karma created. It is for this reason that I have given up eating steamed fish! Not only does it bring me bad luck, it also creates negative karma.

The lotus for purity of thought and intention

The lotus is a symbol of purity and perfection. In Buddhism, the lotus also signifies the attainment of Enlightenment. Its petals are said to symbolize the doctrine of Buddha's teachings. Buddha Himself is usually depicted seated on a sacred lotus. His posture with a straight back and with

The Buddha Shakyamuni seated on a lotus and assuming the lotus posture.

the lower limbs folded in front is called the *lotus posture*.

Buddhist monks and holy Masters all assume this posture when they meditate and teach the sutras. Dharma students also sit in the lotus posture when meditating or taking teachings. Those unused to this cramped position of the lower limbs are usually advised to practice sitting thus, as this is the posture most conducive to generating body quiet, thereby aiding the meditation process. A straight back is also said to encourage the flow of *chi* within the body.

The mantra of the Compassionate Buddha - *Om Mani Peh Meh Hone* - is the lotus mantra and reciting it many thousands of times bring a rain of blessings. The Chinese manifestation of the Compassionate Buddha is the Goddess of Mercy Kuan Yin and this mantra is thus the Kuan Yin mantra.

The Buddha who brought Buddhism to Tibet is called the Lotus Buddha because he is said to have been born from a lotus. In Tibet, he is more popularly known as *Guru Padmasambhava* and He is sometimes also referred to as *Guru Rinpoche*, but to the Chinese, he is called the Lotus Buddha.

Lotus candles will bless your home with happiness and good fortune. Display in the Southwest to activate Love Luck. Place in the South for uninterrupted social advancements.

The canopy is a powerful symbol of protection

The canopy has the significance and meaning of the flag, the banner and the umbrella; as a result of which, it is sometimes drawn as one of these three items. The canopy symbolizes victory in a Buddhist sense, where the real enemy is said to be the selfish ego. The canopy is one of the auspicious signs because Buddhists believe that the successful conquest of man's egos represent one of the most important preliminary steps on the path towards gaining the peerless state of Enlightenment.

On a more mundane level, the canopy takes on the significance of the imperial umbrella. It is a token of someone held in the highest respect. It is a symbol of dignity and high rank. Thus we can say that in a way, the canopy or umbrella represents victory and success in career.

The umbrella is also a symbol of protection from negative influences. The belief is that the placement of an umbrella just outside the front door protects the house from burglars and from strangers with ill intentions.

Umbrellas made of silk, decorated with tassels and painted with auspicious signs when placed inside the house are also said to afford good protection. Such umbrellas should be placed diagonal to the front door.

In Thailand, which is a very Buddhist country, the art of umbrella-making has reached great heights. Exquisite umbrellas, which make good decorations with good meanings that are made of bamboo and paper can be purchased in the northern city of Chiang Mai.

Umbrellas also feature in wedding rituals. It is believed that when the man marries, a silk umbrella should be held over his head as he walks towards the bride. This will ensure that after marriage he will gain high rank and honour. This is because usually only very high dignitaries and important people have umbrellas held over them.

Meanwhile, another umbrella ritual said to be very lucky and protective is that when held over a woman in labour it ensures the safe delivery of the child. This can be a symbolic ritual involving the use of a silk umbrella.

The vase for accumulating happiness and merit

The vase is a symbol of peace and harmony and the placement of flowers in a vase, depending what kind of flowers they are, give rise to a plethora of rich symbolic meanings. As one of the eight auspicious Buddhist objects, the vase symbolizes a receptacle of the blessings of Buddha, manifested in the form of pure nectar and white light. The vase brings peace of mind and also happiness.

From a feng shui viewpoint, a large vase has several uses. If it is used to contain flowers then it is a good thing to place

When you purchase vases and urns, be careful that you do not purchase the variety that is used for keeping the ashes and bones of ancestors. These are seldom made in fine porcelain. Nor will they be in lacquer or bronze.

Instead they are usually earthenware urns that are at least two to three feet high. These are usually called *bone vases*, and are not suitable for keeping flowers or for making into wealth vases. They usually look something like the urn shown here. One way to make sure is to buy a vase that has an open mouth, rather than one with a cap as shown.

four season flowers in it - in any combination whatsoever so as to create peace all year round for the household. These flowers need not be real. They can be made of silk - peonies for summer, chrysanthemums for autumn, orchids for winter and the plum blossoms for spring. Filled with a stalk each of the pine or bamboo, it means a long and peaceful life. Filled with three symbolic halberds, it means successfully (and peacefully) climbing the career ladder. The vase can also be transformed into a wealth vase and this has been covered elsewhere in the book under symbols of wealth and prosperity. Vases that contain auspicious symbols can be placed anywhere in the house except the kitchen. Ideally also fresh flowers should not be placed in bedrooms.

The wheel to be blessed with real wisdom and knowledge

The sacred wheel is one of the auspicious signs believed to be on the footprints of Buddha. It is variously referred to as the Wheel of Life, the Wheel of Truth, the Wheel of a Thousand Spokes and the Wheel of the Cosmos. It symbolizes the noble and wisdom truths of Buddha's teachings. Some say the Wheel symbolizes the Buddha Himself and that it is the Holy one who drew the wheel with grains of rice taken from the rice field. The spokes of the Wheel represent rays of sacred light emanating from the Buddha himself. *The turning of the wheel* represents Buddha's doctrines, or Dharma, being taught by lineage teachers, called gurus or

lamas. In Mahayana Buddhism, especially the Mahayana Buddhism of Tibet, lineage lamas are regarded to be emanations of, and inseparable from, all the Buddhas.

Thus His Holiness Dalai Lama is regarded as an emanation of the Compassionate Buddha, known as Avalokiteshvara in India and Nepal, as Chenresig in Tibet and as the Goddess of Mercy **Kuan Yin** amongst the Chinese.

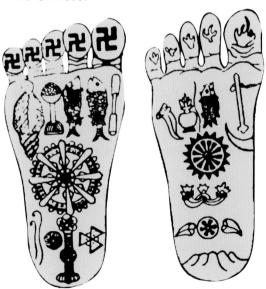

The sacred Wheel of Dharma is shown below left on both feet of Buddha's foot prints. On one foot, the wheel is drawn with eight spokes and on the other foot, it is drawn with symbolically a thousand spokes.

From a feng shui perspective, the wheel represents the inner feng shui of the mind. The wheel signifies overcoming **the three poisons** of existence. These three poisons are ignorance, anger and attachment - considered to be the three root causes of human suffering. The Wheel thus symbolizes the conquest of suffering by overcoming the three poison arrows that cause these sufferings for human beings! Placing the wheel symbol in the house signifies getting peace of mind and growth in wisdom. It is particularly suitable for those looking for the real meaning of life's existence.

The jar for containing valuable relics is a religious symbol

The jar looks like a vase with a cover, not unlike the urn that is used as a receptacle for keeping the relics of ancestors. In the case of the auspicious jar, this is deemed to contain the holy relics of saints and high lamas. These relics are valued highly by Buddhists who regard the jar, the receptacle for such relics as an auspicious object. This is a symbol that was also said to have been found on the Buddha's footprints.

I do not view the jar as a feng shui object in the sense of it bringing any material advantage or benefit. As a Buddhist, I value very highly the relics of Buddhist high lamas and I believe that having them kept on my altar bestows huge blessings on my household, and enormously enhances my own practice. This is based not on feng shui but on my own spiritual and religious belief. Placing a jar like this in the house is therefore not necessarily a feng shui recommendation. This symbol is included in this book because it is one of the 8 auspicious objects of Buddhism.

Since Buddhism was widespread in China, all the symbols associated with Buddhist practice have been incorporated into many traditional beliefs, one of which is feng shui. Understanding the background of objects considered to be auspicious should help readers decide on whether or not to place them in their homes.

Used as a Wealth Jar

Aside from the connotations given above, the jar can also be the receptacle for containing the symbolic wealth of the household. Thus you can treat it like a wealth jar, filling it with semi precious stones, pretend gold ingots, old coins and other precious things. Then cover it and keep the jar hidden away in the bedroom. If you plan on having such a wealth jar, choose one with auspicious designs drawn onto the jar. Dragon and bat images are excellent for this purpose.

According to some practitioners, filling a jar with precious things and then burying it in the West side of your garden creates auspicious grounds and this brings about excellent wealth feng shui.

This is similar to having buried treasure in your own backyard.

Eight Auspicious Objects Together Bring Overall Good Fortune

Shown on the next page are the eight auspicious objects of Buddhism combined together into a single symbol. Displaying all eight objects together is believed to bring very complete good fortune to the household, the kind of good fortune that addresses not only the material luck of the family but also the spiritual luck which brings peace of mind and real happiness.

In fact, many Buddhist households display banners and wall hangings that have these eight objects printed or sewn onto them for good luck.

The eight symbols can also be displayed collectively as paintings on walls, or better yet, they can be drawn as eight separate objects and then embroidered onto heavy materials to be used in front of rooms as door coverings, as room dividers and as screens. I place embroidered versions of these 8 objects on either side of my front door to welcome in the good sheng chi.

As a feng shui tool, wall hangings which have these eight objects make excellent antidotes for overcoming the bad feng shui of doors being placed one

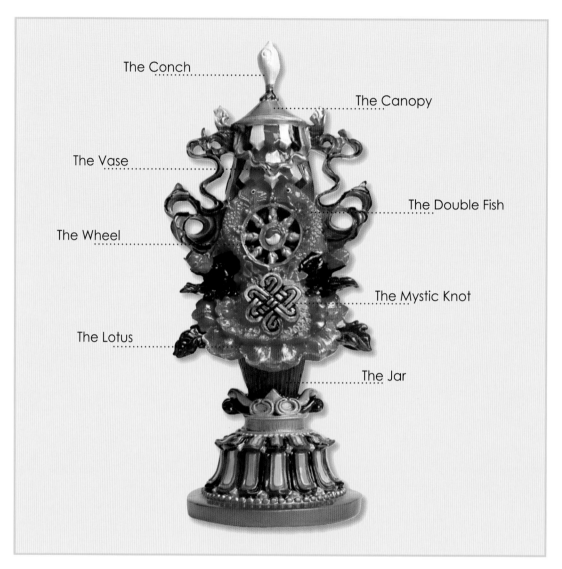

The Conch

The Canopy

The Vase

The Double Fish

The Wheel

The Mystic Knot

The Lotus

The Jar

after another in a straight line. Used this way, it becomes a door curtain which causes fast moving *shar chi* or killing breath to slow down and turn auspicious. When a room divider of some kind is required, one can also use wall hangings embroidered with these eight objects. Thus if your door is too close to the staircase for example, use a door hanging with the 8 objects to overcome the bad chi.

Chapter Eight:
The Eight Precious Treasures

The eight precious treasures of feng shui overlap the eight auspicious objects of the preceding chapter, but under this category, they symbolize prosperity and abundance of material possessions, manifested in eight different ways. Thus the **precious vase** here means the wealth vase filled with precious gems and items of great value that symbolize the wealth of the well-endowed matriarch who keeps the wealth vase hidden for the family.

Then there is the **precious wheel** of knowledge that signifies attainments of scholarship up to the highest levels. These two objects overlap the eight Buddhist treasures already covered in the previous section. The **precious jewel** signifies all the manifestations of great wealth. This can be the diamond, crystal or any of the precious stones. The **precious queen** signifies the powerful matriarch. The **precious general**, usually signified by the God of War Kuan Kung, takes care of defenses

and security against those who would do you ill - he is the protector of your space. It can also be any symbol of a high military official.

The **precious minister** takes care of all civilian matters and ensures that there is peace and prosperity. The **precious horse** brings recognition, fame and the spread of your good name. The **precious elephant** brings an abundance of male heirs and good descendants luck. In Thailand, the elephant is a much loved and revered animal.

These eight precious objects are part of the Mandala offering contained in Buddhist prayers. The mandala offering is itself a most auspicious symbol to have in the home.

The precious jewel to signify all the manifestations of great wealth

The best symbol of the precious jewel is the diamond, and there are beautiful imitations of diamond fashioned out of reconstituted quartz crystal that can be displayed in the home to attract wealth luck. Feng shui belief in the efficacy of the jewel comes from it being one of the eight precious treasures said to be mentally created, and then included in *Mandala* offerings. The origin of *Mandala* offerings are found in Buddhism and Hinduism, and in many of these temples, stunning mandalas made of coloured sand are created for various rituals and *puja* ceremonies. Place a crystal jewel - cut and fashioned into the shape of a diamond - in the Southwest of your hall or bedroom to simulate wealth luck in relationships, and in the Northeast for wealth luck in your studies and education. Place in the West or Northwest for prosperity.

The Magic Square pendant

Jade

To the Chinese, however, the precious jewel is their favourite gemstone, jade, which occurs from white to all shades of green, with the most precious and hence most valuable being jade of a translucent green colour. Jade is considered extremely lucky to wear for good fortune. Because of this, jade has been widely used to decorate belts and head dresses as insignias of high rank. Worn on the body, jade symbolizes protection against illness and poor health. Jade is also believed to strengthen the physical constitution of anyone wearing it. Thus matriarchs were extremely fond of wearing jade bangles on the hands, since this ensured that the cool jade surface would be in constant contact with their skin.

Beautiful carvings of auspicious objects are also made out of jade to enhance their symbolic meanings. Patriarchs celebrating any of their auspicious birthdays - sixty, seventy or eighty - will benefit enormously from receiving the gift of a *jade rod*, a powerful symbol of virility; or other symbols of longevity which have been carved out of jade. The most popular of these symbols is the peach. Done in jade, it is both exquisite and auspicious.

The God of Heaven is also referred to as the *Jade Emperor* and this does suggest that the precious jewel itself has long been regarded as possessing divine attributes and qualities.

The precious queen symbolizes the spirit of the Matriarch

The precious Queen epitomizes the essence and spirit of the Matriarch. It is a powerful symbol and hanging pictures of any Queen familiar to you always creates good energy chi for the mother and female members of the family. In Chinese culture, the Queen almost always refers to the legendary Taoist Queen of Heaven, who is sometimes referred to as the patron Goddess of sailors because she is believed to ensure good weather and safe conduct for their journeys on the high seas. She is known as *Ma Tsu Po*. The precious Queen is also part of the Buddhist Mandala offering and in this context, she can be viewed as the matriarchal equivalent of the emperor. Thus it is considered excellent feng shui to display images of her in the home.

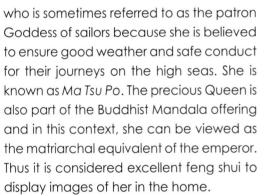

The sector to activate is the Southwest, since this is the place of the trigram *kun* which signifies the essence of the matriarchal spirit.

References to the Queen can also refer to *"Hsi Wang Mu - the Queen of the West"*. Her image in the home is said to bring enormously good fortune.

This Queen is the royal legendary lady believed to reside in the paradise realm located high up in the *Kun Lun*

Mountains. She is usually shown seated on a phoenix and accompanied by two hand maidens.

One waves a large magic fan, and the other carries a tray of immortal peaches that grow in her gardens. This image brings good fortune for many years.

The Precious General secures the household against all the ill winds

Almost all cultures have their military heroes. The equivalent of China's precious generals are the heroes of the Three Kingdoms period of China's history. In feng shui, the military leader symbolizes the guardian who protects against all the ill winds that blow against the household. Shown overleaf is the most famous general in Chinese history - the general Kuan Ti, later known as Kuan Kung, and deified as the God of War. Kuan Kung eventually also became the God of Wealth. Thus he wears many hats, and is a

Place such an image fairly high up (hence not on the coffee table). The precious general should be placed on a vantage point from where he can survey the entrance into the home. If possible, let him stand directly in front of the front door and facing it. It is more meaningful when the figure of the general is armed. Thus, when we display statues of Kuan Kung, we always make sure that he has his sword with him. Military generals on horseback also have good meanings, but do not let the horse be pointing directly at the door.

most useful personage to have in the house. Placing his image in the home, especially when directly facing the front door, ensures that his fierce countenance will scare away all the bad things and any killing breath that may be coming through the door. It is believed that all energy that is negative does not enter into the presence of Kuan Kung. His two other brothers, meanwhile, are also regarded as auspicious figurines to have in the house.

Those of you who are wary of placing Chinese deities in your home could consider placing the figurine of a military figure that symbolizes bravery, courage and fearlessness. He can then represent the precious general for you. If you are British, you can have the hero of Waterloo. If you are French, you can have Napoleon Bonaparte. If you are American, you can have General Eisenhower, Colin Campbell or any one of your own war heroes. The idea is to have the essence and presence of a military leader.

The *Precious Minister* ensures there is peace and prosperity

When a household is well managed, there will be harmony and prosperity. The presence of the *Precious Minister* implies this state of affairs. His presence further implies the following types of luck :

- To start with, the family will benefit from a powerful and successful Patriarch who is highly regarded in the corridors of power. The Precious Minister is deemed to be both the benefactor and the patron of the house.

- Secondly, it suggests that the family is wealthy and will have the ability to maintain its lifestyle and residence. The implication therefore is good fortune that is both long lasting and consistent.

- Thirdly, the precious Minister ensures there will always be harmony in the household, and this implies good feelings and loyalty between siblings as well as between the various women folk who live under the same roof. In the old days where there were secondary wives as well as unmarried sisters living together in the same household, household harmony and peace were always one of the hallmarks of a home with good feng shui.

Pau Kung

- Fourthly, the precious Minister symbolizes all the noblest qualities of the *superior man*. These qualities and attributes are deemed also be in the sons of the family, thereby aiding them to gain success.

I have in my home a particularly good ceramic sculpture of *Pao Kung* - the judge famed for his wisdom of judgements. To me he signifies success with principles. Family patriarchs who have been honored with high awards should display photographs of the patriarch in full regalia in the home. Pictures taken with Ministers are good feng shui and these should be prominently displayed in the living room, either on sideboards or on top of the piano. Also when you display the symbolic presence of powerful men (and women) in your house, the badge of power and success permeates the environment in a very positive way.

The Precious Horse stands for endurance, loyalty & purity

The horse is the seventh creature of the Chinese Zodiac. In Buddhist texts, it stands for endurance, loyalty and purity. It is precious when it is depicted laden with precious things. Then it expresses the aspiration of a comfortable life and the attainment of high rank, which brings recognition, and a life of comfort. The horse illustrated here is a precious horse on whose back is laden beautiful precious offerings.

The **tribute horse** is an auspicious variation of this same idea. In feng shui, the horse symbolizes yang energy and its representative direction on the Zodiac is the South. When you wish to fully activate the energies of the South, one of the best ways of doing so is to place a tribute horse or precious horse in that corner of the house. There are beautiful horses carved out of jade and ivory and some of these are decorated with precious gemstones. These are true symbols of the precious horse and by placing them in the south part of the home, you will be energizing the luck of recognition. Those wanting to do well in their careers, particularly those who want their talents and hard work to be recognized by the right people should place just such a symbol in the South.

Tribute Horse Ring

When would you want to energize the South?

• Firstly, when the South is one of your four good directions under the KUA formula Eight Mansions School of Feng Shui (please refer to my Compass formula book "*8 Mansions Feng Shui*" for the formula). Each person according to the KUA formula has four good and four bad directions. It is extremely useful to find out what these directions are. If South is a good direction, you should energize it.

• Secondly, when the flying stars of your South sector are deemed to be auspicious (please refer to my book, FLYING STAR FENG SHUI for PERIOD 8 for the formula to cast the flying star chart of your house).

• Thirdly, when you wish to energize the aspirations represented by the South, which is fame, recognition and gaining a good reputation.

The *Precious Elephant* is said to have the strength to hold up the world

The elephant is one of the precious holy animals of Buddhism and in Thailand, the precious elephant has always been strongly associated with the country's image. In Burma too, the elephant is accorded special status. Buddha is said to have been conceived by entering his mother's side as a white elephant and thus till this day, sightings of **white elephants** are always regarded as good luck omens. Meanwhile, according to Hindu mythology, the world is believed to be resting on the back of an elephant who stands atop

a tortoise, and one of the most powerful and popular Gods of Hinduism, the **Lord Ganesh** is depicted as an elephant.

Mahayana Buddhists of China frequently represent the elephant with a lotus flower on its back, upon which is seated the Buddha of Wisdom known as *Pu Hsien Pu Sart* in Chinese and the Buddha Manjushuri in Tibetan. The precious elephant is also regarded as the bearer of the **wish granting jewel,** as well as the **sacred begging bowl** of the Buddha. The Thais have adopted the white elephant as the country's national symbol, believing it to be an emanation of a future Buddha.

In Asia, therefore, the elephant is accorded divine status, and those Buddhists belonging to the older generation even consider it a symbol of universal sovereignty. There is something infinitely good and benign about the elephant image. Many place miniature images of the elephant on the altar as an offering to Buddha, believing it to symbolize many good things. If you wish to display the precious elephant in your home as a symbol of good fortune, it is a good idea to place a basket of precious things on its back, since this denotes the elephant bringing these auspicious objects into the home. Place a pair of elephants near the vicinity of the front door either inside or outside the house.

You can place flowering plants or anything else deemed auspicious on top of the elephant. He is said to have the strength and energy to hold up the world!

The elephant is a sacred symbol of fertility and for descendants luck

Along the long avenues leading to the Ming tombs just outside Beijing in China, the tourist can see gigantic stone elephants. These elephants are kneeling, standing and sitting. I took the picture below many years ago when I visited the tombs of the Ming emperors as part of my feng shui education. I had been told that feng shui had played a prominent role in the founding of the Ming dynasty in China, and that all through the reign of the Ming emperors, feng shui experts were frequently consulted at Court. I had also

been told that the Ming tombs located just outside the capital city had been built according to strict feng shui principles, nestled as they were in the embrace of the green dragon and white tiger hills.

I noticed the stone elephants as soon as we entered the avenues that led to the tombs, and my guide informed me that those elephants along the avenue were said to bestow wonderful descendants' luck on anyone touching and stroking them. I was told later on that evening by a feng shui expert that childless couples as well as couples wishing to give birth to boy babies had had their wishes granted after stroking the elephants kneeling along the avenue.

This belief is part superstition and part religious. The elephant being a symbol for getting children originates from the story of Buddha's birth since of course Buddha Shakyamuni was believed to have entered his mother's womb brought by a white elephant. Elephants have since been regarded favourably as symbols of fertility.

Those desperately wanting a child can place the image of a kneeling elephant by their altar and pray for a son. Or they can introduce the elephant image into their bedroom. Place a pair of carved wooden elephants next to the bed.

To make doubly sure that feng shui can indeed help in such a situation, childless couples might also want to try sleeping with their heads pointed to the husband's **nien yen** direction.

All the treasures of the Universe in the *Mandala*

A *Mandala* is such an extremely auspicious symbol. The mandala signifies a pure Universe where all manner of precious things, real as well as created in the mind (imagined) are placed together in concentric circles as special offerings to the Buddhas. Shown below is an elaborately and painstakingly made *sand mandala*. Different colours of specially prepared sand are used to make such a mandala. Placing a mandala like this in one's home is said to be most auspicious. I know that Buddhists of the Mahayana tradition create mandalas like this whenever there is a particularly important puja being conducted or when a special initiation is being done. For instance, whenever His Holiness the Dalai Lama does an initiation after a teaching, his monks and

disciples usually construct an appropriate mandala as an offering. Making the mandala requires skill and craftsmanship. The best mandala makers are monks from India, Nepal and Tibet. The mandala is usually built on a base that has been blessed with incense and fragrance. In the center is placed the symbolic Mount Meru, the Buddhist paradise mountain said to be the center of the world. I have discovered that many cultural traditions refer to a central mountain that is deemed to be the

holy mountain, and in feng shui, mountains play a large part in bringing good chi flows to houses located in auspicious orientation to them.

The holy mountains of China are referred to as the Kunlun Mountains, which are said to be located somewhere near to the Himalayan Mountains.

Perhaps somewhere here in this highest mountain range of the world is Shangri La, or Shambala - the heavens of the Gods and the Buddhas? Whatever the reality, I know that in feng shui, having a solid high mountain behind you and on the left and right of you, thus surrounding you on three sides, is said to be most auspicious. The mandala simulates the central mountain, the four continents, all manner of precious things, the sun and the moon, the precious parasol and the banner of victory. Not surprising as it is so auspicious!

Using the magic of the winds to actualize your wishes

A famous Taoist master from Hong Kong once gave me a wish list ritual, which he said would enhance my business luck.

The ritual:

I was to write down whatever I wanted really badly onto a helium filled balloon. I was to write my wish clearly and succinctly. And then I was to release the balloon and let it fly up high into the sky.

It wasn't feng shui by any means - it was a mind ritual that just seemed to be such fun to do. One Sunday I wrote down my wish to be able to shop like a queen in all the capitals of the world! I wanted to close a business deal for myself that would enable me to love my work. I was fed up of being a banker. I wanted to do something fun, something more feminine! So *I wished for a department store*! That was how I got the Dragon Seed deal, which enabled me to have my own chain of department stores, and enabled me to shop like an Empress for two years when

I was the store's Executive Chairman. Talk about having one's wishes come true. Those years with Dragon Seed, I shopped in all the fashion capitals of the world. I shopped for my chain of stores. I shopped till I dropped.

A variation of the balloon wish list is the *banner of victory* you can tie across your garden. Let the winds carry your wishes into the sky to be actualized for you. Years later, when I met my precious holy Lama, he told me about *prayer flags* and explained how each time the winds wafted over holy mantras printed on the flags, they blessed all beings touched by the same wind. He reminded me of my balloons except His was a far more beautiful way of using the magic of the wind. I thought I'd share this little tidbit with you!

Chapter Nine:
Feng Shui Prosperity Enhancers

The four objects that are said to attract great good fortune into any home are the **wish granting tree**, the **wish fulfilling cow**, the **unharvested harvest** and the **precious mountain**. Old paintings of these subjects are highly valued especially when they have been hanging in the home of a rich family. The wish granting tree is what gave rise to the gem tree which is enjoying a huge revival of popularity - ever since South Africa started exporting beautiful "gem trees" made of a variety of semi-precious stones.

The wish fulfilling cow has always been a great favourite with Chinese landowners. In India, of course, the cow is regarded as a holy animal. The precious mountain is believed to be a repository of great wealth (as in *the mountain is gold*). Other popular feng shui enhancers include the ever popular **windchimes** which energize the West and the Northwest, wealth bringing **water features** which enhance the luck of the East, the Southeast and the North, and bright yang energy **lights** and chandeliers that magnify the luck of the South.

Plant a wish granting tree in the East

Trees play an extremely important role in the practice of feng shui. As a deflector of bad energy, they can be quite excellent tools for overcoming the onslaught of killing chi. Thus if your front door is being "hit" by poison arrows from across the road, plant a bushy tree to completely block out the *arrow* from view. These *arrows* can be straight roads, the triangular rooflines of houses across the road or they can be anything sharp, straight or hostile. Sometimes, even the edges of big buildings can create the bad energy of poison arrows. All these hostile structures that bring ill fortune and bad luck can be completely deflected by planting and positioning a tree in a strategic spot that enables the source of the arrow to be blocked off from view.

But the tree is even more effective when it is planted at a spot in the garden that transforms it into the *wish granting tree*. According to feng shui texts, the potency of the tree in bringing auspicious good fortune depends on 3 things:

- Firstly, it depends on the exact spot where it is planted.

- Secondly, it depends on what type of tree it is.

- Thirdly, it depends on what is done to energize the wealth prospects of the tree.

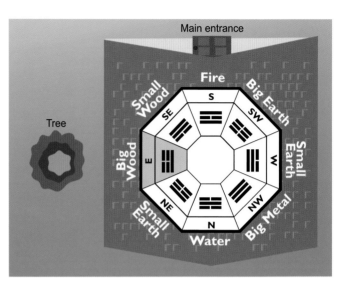

Main entrance

Tree

It is best to plant the tree in the East and to find the exact spot, take the directions from the center of the house and then measure the 45 degrees that represent the East from the center. The tree should be in this quadrant (see sketch). Next, select a bushy tree, preferably one with rounded leaves. Finally, hang a thousand coins tied together with red thread and let it hang from the tree. Think of this tree as the wish granting tree!

Place the wish fulfilling cow in the Southeast

I am very fond of telling people the story of my *wish fulfilling cow*. It was a crystal ornament presented to me by my staff at the Dao Heng Bank in Hong Kong where I was Managing Director in the early Eighties. But it was not a cow, it was a bull, and it had beautiful specks of 24 carat gold sprinkled inside it. I placed it in a place of honour in the living room of my home, and it brought me a great deal of wealth luck!

The cow is considered an extremely holy animal in places like India and Nepal.

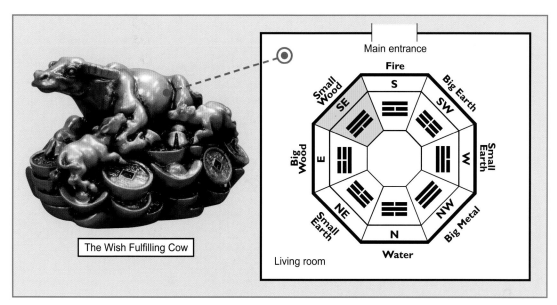

The Wish Fulfilling Cow

But few realize the true significance of the cow. According to Buddhist teachings, the cow has the power to transform your wishes into reality provided you treat it with kindness; and provided also that you refrain from eating beef. It is for this reason that so many Chinese who are Buddhists refrain from eating cow meat or beef! In India, if you knock into a cow and kill it, you can be charged with manslaughter; and in Katmandu, cows roam the streets freely because they know they will not get knocked down. Killing a cow with your motor vehicle there can cause you to be imprisoned for murder! This is because the cow is considered to be such a sacred animal!

In feng shui, the wish fulfilling cow is so potent that practitioners place the image of a cow relaxing on a bed of coins. But if you do not have this symbol, then look for a painting which includes the cow and hang it in the southeast to energize for the wealth luck associated with this corner. Use the Pa Kua to identify the SE sector of your living room. Then hang a nice painting with the cow in it, or better yet, place the sculptured image of a cow in this corner. Think of it as the wish fulfilling cow who tills the land, provides transportation, pulls the cart and even provides meat for food.

The cow is said to be a holy animal because it provides so much sustenance for the human race. Thus, rather than eat it, it is better to use its image to enhance one's luck at home.

Display the precious mountain behind you for support & protection

The mountain is said to be the single most important symbol in feng shui simply because the mountain is a manifestation of all four of the celestial creatures of the four directions. This means the Dragon of the East, the Phoenix of the South, the Tortoise of the North and the Tiger of the West. Mountains are also said to have a *yin* and a *yang* aspect; and are also categorized according to shapes that correspond to

the five elements. In general, the mountain is said to represent a wealth of hidden treasure. This is indicated by the trigram **ken** in the I Ching, which describes the mountain as being still, waiting and being prepared.

The mountain contains within it masses of gold and precious things. Thus the precious mountain is a repository of great wealth. When you can see clear mountain peaks in the distance, they are usually indications of various types of good fortune. Thus seeing three mountain peaks in the distance indicates that the eldest son of the family will one day rule the land. Indeed, this is a most powerful omen, especially when it is read with other divinitive signs.

The best way to use the mountain symbol in feng shui is to hang the painting or picture of the mountain behind you at work. This will ensure that in bad economic times you will survive. You will not get laid off. You will not lose out in a political fight within the company. And you will always survive in any strategic one-upmanship in the office. If you are a businessman, you will survive. You will not collapse due to bad times. The mountain offers support and protection.

You will notice that many Chinese businessmen of the old school almost always hang landscape paintings behind them at their place of work. This is to ensure they are always supported by the most powerful symbol on earth. Should you want to do this, please always make sure that there is no water feature in the painting of mountains behind you. Any small waterfall in landscape paintings represents water. These would be unsuitable placed behind you.

Simulate the *about to be harvested* field of corn, rice, wheat

When you enter any upmarket Chinese Arts and Crafts shop you will find images of freshly harvested fruits made of expensive jadeite, ivory or ceramics. This is because these fresh fruits represent the *about-to-be-harvested* produce of the land.

These are extremely auspicious images, and for obvious reasons. They represent the fruit of the land and displaying them anywhere in your home, and especially in your dining room area brings the luck of prosperity for the family. The symbolism is that the family will always have more than enough to eat. For the same reason, I have always recommended hanging beautiful paintings of fresh fruit in the dining room. In feng shui, food signifies prosperity!

The display of fruits freshly plucked from the tree has its origins in the belief that images of *unploughed harvest* are considered to be the luckiest of all food symbols. Thus, paintings of fully matured cornfields, rice fields and wheat fields are excellent for hanging in both homes and offices. In fact, if you are trying to decide on subject matter, look for still life paintings of freshly harvested fruits or of fields of ripe corn and wheat! This is because a field of corn or any other cereal food ripe for the plucking symbolizes the crystallizing of hard work. The time for harvesting is always summer. For this reason, the season of summer represents a flowering and a blooming of efforts. The meanings are most auspicious. Summer is also considered a time of plenty, a time when there is a maximum amount of the precious yang energy. When you compound this with an image of an unharvested harvest about to bear fruit and food, there cannot be any symbolism more powerful!

Hang ever popular windchimes to activate luck in the West & NW

There are several misconceptions about the hanging of windchimes in the home - two in particular that I wish to address.

Firstly, some people have heard that windchimes attract malevolent spirits into the house. I am frequently asked this question in emails sent to me. I want to say that I have hung windchimes in my home now for over twenty years with no problems whatsoever.

My windchimes have brought me nothing but good luck and good fortune.

Secondly, it is important to differentiate between using windchimes to press down on bad luck in certain sectors to overcome a variety of feng shui ills and using windchimes to energize for good luck.

When you use windchimes **to overcome bad luck**, it is a good idea to try and use windchimes that have 5 or 6 rods. Some masters advise that solid rods do a better job of pressing down on bad luck; others maintain that hollow rods are much better, and I agree. More important is that it should be all metal and the addition of a pagoda-like structure above is said to be most effective in frightening any bad spirits that may be lurking around. This is because the pagoda is a powerful symbol of protection against bad spirits. **6 rod hollow windchimes are the best solutions for most flying star afflictions.** Hang windchimes to protect against overhead beams and sharp corners. (For those who have knowledge of flying star feng shui, you can also hang windchimes in sectors where there are bad flying stars in the house natal chart.)

To **energize for good luck**, windchimes work extremely well in the metal element sectors of the house. This of course assumes the use of metal windchimes i.e. windchimes that are made predominantly of metal (eg copper, brass, silver, steel and types of alloys). The metal sectors are the **West** and the **Northwest**. Windchimes are particularly powerful when hung to activate the luck of the patriarch in the Northwest corners of living rooms and offices, and for the luck of health and longevity in the West. For energizing purposes, remember to use only those with hollow rods. Also please note that 6 rods is excellent for the Northwest, and 7 rods is excellent for the West.

Create a water feature in the North, East or Southeast

To benefit from the creation of a water feature in the house, the most important thing to take note of are the following:

- First, water features are things like small ponds, miniature fountains, waterfalls and aquariums.

- Second, water features are different from the *water dragon* as contained in my "Get Rich with Water" book, since these do not address the matter of **flow of water**. Water features are meant only to activate the water element in certain sectors.

- Third, there are three sectors that benefit from the placement of a water feature. These are the East, the Southeast and the North. Of the three, the most beneficial is the North because this sector is representative of the water element. In the East and Southeast, water benefits the wood element of those sectors.

- Fourth, it is advisable not to have water directly behind the house, since this indicates missed opportunities. However, if your North is behind you, you can place a water feature here, except try to orientate it such that it is on either side of the house rather than directly behind the house. If the flying stars indicate *good stars* for the back of the house, then placing a water feature there will be most beneficial. (Flying Star overides).

- Fifth, make very certain that the water feature is not on the right hand side of the main front door. This is taken from the inside looking out. Water features should always be to the left of the main door.

Water features should never overwhelm the house. For this reason, I am always very wary of **swimming pools**, which tend to be always a little too large for a residential home. If yours is a country mansion, then having a swimming pool does not in any way cause an imbalance of energy, in which case the pool will do no harm unless it is in a bad sector. If it is in a good sector, it will be most beneficial.

Despite this, it is a good idea to treat pools with care.

Use lots of yang energy lights to enhance the South

One of the most potent of all symbolic enhancers of good fortune energy are lights - bright lights that bring a huge dose of precious yang energy. Like windchimes, however, lights can be used for a double fold purpose. This is because lights are a most powerful antidote against many feng shui ills. Lights can overcome misplaced toilets to some extent. And lights can dissolve the shar chi created by narrow corridors and tight corners. Usually, for such areas where stagnant chi tend to accumulate, shining a bright light is sufficient to overcome the bad energy.

Lights can also be a powerful counter agent to missing corners. The shining of lights

always means the introduction of life and yang energy. This is usually sufficient to get the *chi* moving again. But it is as feng shui prosperity enhancers that lights become most useful. Thus they can be placed all round a shop or business. This attracts customers and helps to double the turnover of the business.

Lights are excellent when used to energize the South sector/corner of the home or of the living room. These would be even better if red in color. Energizing the South will bring recognition and attract promotion.

Lights are usually great for romance and marriage luck when kept turned on in the Southwest, the place of the matriarch. It is best to have such a light in the garden of the home, and to keep such a light switched on for at least 3 hours each night. To ensure potency of this symbol, create a

light at the end of a pole that has been sunk into the ground. This will symbolically raise the energy of the earth, which will benefit the women of the household. You can use modern electrical light fittings or you can use an old fashioned lantern. Both should work equally well. Although, of course, the light that shines the brightest will attract the stronger yang energy.

The best kind of lighting to use are crystal chandeliers. These light fittings combine two complementary elements - fire and earth - in the process producing masses of *yang* energy that in turn bring in masses of sheng chi. Place a small chandelier just outside the house directly facing the main door. Then place another chandelier inside the house also directly facing the main door. These chandeliers will ensure only the most auspicious *chi* enters!

Chapter Ten:
The Twelve Animals of the Zodiac

The twelve animals of the Chinese Zodiac symbolize the earthly branches. Each of the animals, starting from the Rat and ending with the Boar, has a corresponding compass direction, which offers very specific guidelines on where to place images of these animals to magnify the energy and symbolic attributes of these animals. The directions of the animal signs also offer vital clues on the "*danger*" sectors in the home in each year. Thus, while it is auspicious to place images of the *animal* in their respective home sectors, it is also useful to check against the general horoscope fortunes based on astrological readings.

More important is to take note of the *flying star feng shui* taboos in each year, and to note how these affect each of the animal signs. The table below is a very valuable table. It summarizes where the three danger sectors are for each year. These are sectors that are occupied by the *Grand Duke Jupiter*, the *Three Killings* and the *Deadly Five Yellow*. Meanwhile, the text in this chapter gives specific symbolic feng shui solutions for each year's taboo sectors for every animal sign. Study this chapter carefully.

Year	Animal Sign or Earthly Branch	Place of Deadly Five Yellow (45°)	Place of Three Killings (90°)	Place of Grand Duke Jupiter (15°)
2007	BOAR	Northeast	West	Northwest 3
2008	RAT	South	South	North
2009	OX	North	East	Northeast 1
2010	TIGER	Southwest	North	Northeast 3
2011	RABBIT	East	West	East
2012	DRAGON	Southeast	South	Southeast 1
2013	SNAKE	Center	East	Southeast 3
2014	HORSE	Northwest	North	South
2015	SHEEP	West	West	Southwest 1
2016	MONKEY	Northeast	South	Southwest 3
2017	ROOSTER	South	East	West
2018	DOG	North	North	Northwest 1

The lunar calendar

The Chinese calendar is made up of 60 year cycles that are differentiated according to *heavenly stems* and *earthly branches*. There are ten stems and twelve branches. In the 60 year cycle, the stems comprise the 5 elements with a *yin* or a *yang* aspect (hence 5 X 2 = 10 stems). The 12 stems refer to the animal signs. This system of stems and branches comprehensively symbolizes the interaction between heaven and earthly forces and they are supposed to both reflect and determine the destiny of mankind. Thus all divination and fortune telling methods ultimately rely on the correct interpretations of the personal stems and branches of any individual. These stems and branches can also be used to personalize the feng shui of any individual and this section of the book directly addresses this.

Every person has their own stems and branches and this can be determined from the 100 years calendar given at the back of the book. Use the calendar and check against your **western** date of birth. The calendar at the back of the book is a simplified calendar. It does not enable you to calculate your Eight Characters since that requires also the time and day of your birth. However, for the purposes of using the stems and branches to practise symbolic feng shui, those calculations are not necessary.

All you require is to determine:

1. The **element** of your **heavenly stem** in your year of birth

2. The **animal sign** (and its corresponding **element**) of your year of birth. This will be your **earthly branch** from which you will be able to select symbols that are auspicious for you, and you will also be able to identify the specific location in the home to place these symbols.

It is useful to learn how to take compass directions from the center of the house. Mark out the compass sector that corresponds to your animal sign to the exact degree. Each animal sign is said to occupy 30 degrees of the compass total of 360 degrees. Learn to mark out the sector that represents your animal sign in your house. If you do not know how to read a compass, get someone to teach you before attempting to do it yourself. Invest in a good compass. Any western style compass is fine. Do not flip or reverse directions when applying.

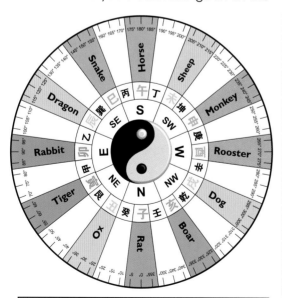

The 12 Zodiac signs and their corresponding directions

The RAT
1912, 1924, 1936, 1948, 1960, 1972, 1984, 1996

The Rat is the first sign of the Chinese Zodiac. Its intrinsic element is **water.** The hour of the RAT is said to be between **11.00 pm to 1.00 am** in the morning. So anyone born at midnight is said to be born in the hour of the Rat. The compass direction of the Rat is between **337.5 degrees to 7.5 degrees.** This falls in the direction of North. You will find that this sector of the house occupies an angle of 30 degrees. This sector is said to be the part of the house deemed very lucky for those residents who are born in any of the years of the Rat. The years of the Rat are listed above.

These years have not however been adjusted to take account of the lunar New Year. Thus if you were born in any of the above years but during say, the month of January, chances are you do not belong to the Rat year but instead to the year prior to the Rat year, which is the year of the Boar. In the same way, you could still be a Rat if you were born in the January of the following year. To check your date of birth against the lunar calendar, please refer to the 100-year lunar calendar at the back of the book.

To energize good wealth luck into your personal earthly branch sector, here are several symbolic things you can do:

· You can place the metaphorical precious mongoose which looks like a Rat in the sector of your house that lies between the degrees indicated for the Rat direction, or any kind of image of the Rat in this part of the house.

· You can activate the same sector with a **water feature** since this is the intrinsic element of your animal sign. It would however be quite bad luck if your sector (i.e. North) were afflicted with a toilet placed there or a kitchen placed there since this would cause your personalized sector to become negatively affected.

· Because your animal sign is the Rat, two other sectors are deemed excellent for you and these correspond to the animal years of the Dragon and the Monkey. The direction of the Dragon is East-Southeast and the direction of the Monkey is West-Southwest.

General Luck of the RAT in Different Years
Those born in the year of the RAT are advised to observe the following:

In the year 2007
Not a good year. Need to lie low. This is year when you require protection. Place a blue rhinoceros in the North sector to keep the robbery star under control.

In the year 2008
Great year for speculative luck and gambling. Hang 8 immortal coins or 6 big emperor coins in the North to bring in the heaven luck. This is the year to invest for business.

In the year 2009
Misfortune luck is located in your sector. Place a 5 element pagoda in the North to control the 5 yellow. Also wear the Om syllable to protect you from harm and mishaps.

In the year 2010
A moderately good year. Romance luck is on your side. Get your peach blossom animal, the Rooster, and place in the west sector. Single Rats will find their true love.

In the year 2011
The Rat will face some argumentative and legal entanglements this year. Avoid too much noise in the North sector. Keep this part of the house as quite as possible. Place a ksiddigarbha staff here.

In the year 2012
The Rat continues to suffer some bad fortune. Display a Wu Lou by the bedside to ensure there is no illness and sickness due to the illness star presence. Do more exercise and eat healthy food.

Water Feature

In the year 2013
Rat people enjoy a good period with no major problems of any kind. Place a water feature in the North to bring you good career and success luck.

In the year 2014
The Rat enjoys excellent fame and recognition luck. Your fame luck will be even better if you display a phoenix in the South of your home to bring you honours.

In the year 2015
The Rat continues to enjoy good fortune. 6 tier waterfall or aquarium in the North will ensure you enjoy good income and wealth luck. Strengthen wealth luck in the SW with a money plant.

In the year 2016
The Rat faces financial losses, and possibility of robbery and thief. Must have a pair of Fu Dogs at the entrance of your main door. Carry with you a blue aventurine rhinoceros.

In the year 2017
The Rat's fortunes recover. You are poised for growth. Place a three-legged toad pulling coins or a bowl of ingots and coins to enhance prosperity luck.

In the year 2018
This is bad year. Rats face misfortune luck and possibility of loss of money, loss of relationships or loss of career status. Must have 6 rod metal windchime in the North to guard against the five yellow.

The OX
1913, 1925, 1937, 1949, 1961, 1973, 1985, 1997

The Ox is the second sign of the Chinese Zodiac. Its intrinsic element is **earth.** The hour of the Ox is said to be between **1.00 am to 3.00 am** in the morning. So anyone born between those hours is said to be born in the hour of the OX. The compass direction of the Ox is between **7.5 degrees to 37.5 degrees.** This falls in the direction of North-Northeast.

You will find that this sector of the house occupies an angle of 30 degrees. This sector is said to be the part of the house deemed very lucky for those residents who are born in any of the years of the Ox. The years of the Ox are listed above. These years have not been adjusted to take account of the lunar New Year. Thus if you were born in any of the above years but during say, the month of January, chances are, you do not belong to the Ox year but instead to the year prior to the Ox year which is the year of the Rat. In the same way, you could still be an Ox if you were born in the January of the following year. To check your date of birth against the lunar calendar, please refer to the 100-year lunar calendar at the back of the book.

To energize good wealth luck into your personal earthly branch sector, here are several symbolic things you can do:

- Place the symbolic wish-fulfilling cow in the sector of your house that lies between the degrees indicated for the Ox, or use any image of a cow, bull or anything belonging to this family in this part of the house. The best images would be made of ceramic, crystal or other materials which belong to the earth element.

- You can activate the same sector with any **earth element feature** since this is the intrinsic element of your animal sign. It would however bring bad luck if your sector (i.e. North-Northeast) were afflicted with a toilet or a kitchen, since this would cause your personalized sector to become negatively affected.

- Because your animal sign is the Ox, two other sectors are deemed excellent for you and these correspond to the animal years of the Snake and the Rooster. The direction of the Snake is South-Southeast and the direction of the Rooster is West.

General Luck of the OX in Different Years
Those born in the year of the OX are advised to observe the following:

In the year 2007
Not a good year. Time to lie low. Will benefit from protective symbols. Place Fu Dogs flanking the front door and a 5 Element Pagoda in the Northeast.

Fu Dogs

In the year 2008
A year of romance. Place a pair of birds in the Southwest corner of your bedroom to enjoy good relationship luck.

In the year 2009
Control your temper and stay low profile. Avoid arguements and quarrels with others. You will lose in most battles. Carry an 18K gold apple pendant to help you.

In the year 2010
Confidence levels decrease this year. Place a metal windchime wu lou in the Northeast and display a Longevity God in the East to promote good health.

In the year 2011
A mixed year. The Ox will benefit greatly if they place a ru yi in the office or at the work place to enhance authority luck.

In the year 2012
The Ox enjoys promotion luck. Get a monkey on horse and place in the South sector of your office or house to bring recognition luck.

In the year 2013
A year of abundant good fortune. Place coins, three legged toads and water features in the Northeast to bring money and wealth luck.

In the year 2014
The Ox enters a bad period. Avoid going out too late at night and watch your money and surroundings while walking alone. Carry a protective amulet coin to safeguard from harm.

In the year 2015
Heaven luck is on your side. Enjoy yourself in this year. Get money or gem trees as this magnifies your good luck.

In the year 2016
The Ox experiences troubled times. It is a good idea to use the metal element to enhance in the Northeast area of your house.

In the year 2017
Good family luck. Excellent education luck. Magnify with Dragon carps. Dragon carps are good for those just started working or still studying.

In the year 2018
A very unsettling time. Emotional and family problems prevail. Counter this by placing 6 crystal balls in the center of the house.

The TIGER
1914, 1926, 1938, 1950, 1962, 1974, 1986, 1998

The TIGER is the third sign of the Chinese Zodiac. Its intrinsic element is **wood.** The hour of the Tiger is said to be between **3.00 am to 5.00 am** in the morning. So anyone born between those hours is said to be born in the hour of the Tiger. The compass direction of the Tiger is between **37.5 degrees to 67.5 degrees.** This falls in the direction of East-Northeast.

You will find that this sector of the house occupies an angle of 30 degrees. This sector is said to be the part of the house deemed very lucky for residents born in any of the years of the Tiger. The years of the Tiger are listed above. These years have not been adjusted to take account of the lunar New Year. Thus if you were born in any of the above years but during say, the month of January, chances are, you do not belong to the Tiger year but instead to the year prior to the Tiger year which is the year of the Ox. In the same way, you could still be a Tiger if you were born in the January of the following year. To check your date of birth against the lunar calendar, please refer to the 100-year lunar calendar at the back of the book.

To energize good wealth luck into your personal **earthly branch** sector, here are several symbolic things you can do:

- Place images of the Tiger in the sector of your house that lies between the degrees indicated above. Since your animal sign is that of the Tiger, you will benefit from the Tiger image. To enhance its intrinsic energy, display wooden carvings or sculptures of the Tiger. This energizes the wood element and is beneficial.

- Activate the same sector with any **wood element feature** since this is the intrinsic element of your animal sign. It will however be bad luck if your sector (i.e. East-Northeast) is afflicted with a toilet or a kitchen since this would cause your personalized sector to become negatively affected.

- Because your animal sign is the Tiger, two other sectors deemed excellent for you are those that correspond to the animal years of the Horse and the Dog. The direction of the Horse is South and the direction of the Dog is West-Northwest.

General Luck of the TIGER in Different Years
Those born in the year of the TIGER are advised to observe the following:

In the year 2007
A bad year for Tiger people. Do not overwork or stress yourself out. Wear an 18k gold 5 element pagoda to protect you from bad luck.

In the year 2008
Good relationship luck. This is the time to look for your future partner. Continue to enhance with feng shui energizers and add your peach blossom animals.

In the year 2009
This is the year to stay quiet and low profile. Go for holiday and enjoy yourself. Install a glitter lamp in the Northeast to help control the bad energy.

In the year 2010
Tiger year people should watch their health and take things easy this year. Place a longevity God in the East sector to ensure your health does not suffer.

In the year 2011
Fortunes improve. Have the 3 Emperors in the Northwest of your office. This will smoothen everything for you and bring success luck.

In the year 2012
This is an exceptionally good year. Place a phoenix and victory horse in the South of your house to magnify good luck.

In the year 2013
Plenty of money luck. Enhance with coins and fish features. Attend auspicious parties and weddings as frequently as possible to bring yang energy that will help you.

In the year 2014
A slight reversal of fortunes. Protect with a pair of Rhinoceros flanking your main door.

In the year 2015
The Tiger benefits from help and support from powerful patrons. Energize the NW sector with a 8 rod metal winchime.

In the year 2016
This will be a year of disappointments and setbacks when the Tiger must be protected against misfortune. This is the year to plan your schedule carefully.

In the year 2017
Tigers will enjoy good social relationships this year. Activate your SW sector with love birds to meet good friends.

In the year 2018
The Tiger extends his run of bad luck. Control with relevant feng shui cures and add a Ksiddigarbha staff in the Northeast.

3 Emperors

The RABBIT
1915, 1927, 1939, 1951, 1963, 1975, 1987, 1999

The Rabbit is the fourth sign of the Chinese Zodiac. Its intrinsic element is **wood**. The hour of the Rabbit is said to be between **5.00 am to 7.00 am** in the early morning. Anyone born between those hours is said to be born in the hour of the Rabbit. The compass direction of the Rabbit is between **67.5 degrees to 97.5 degrees**. This falls in the direction of the East.

You will find that this sector of the house occupies an angle of 30 degrees. This sector is said to be the part of the house deemed very lucky for those residents who are born in any of the years of the Rabbit. The years of the Rabbit are listed above. These years have not been adjusted to take account of the lunar New Year. Thus if you were born in any of the above years but during say, the month of January, chances are, you do not belong to the Rabbit year but instead to the year prior to the Rabbit year which is the year of the Tiger. In the same way, you could still be a Rabbit if you were born in the January of the following year. To check your date of birth against the lunar calendar, please refer to the 100 year lunar calendar at the back of the book.

To energize good wealth luck into your personal **earthly branch** sector, here are several symbolic things you can do:

....

• You can place images of the Rabbit in the sector of your house that lies between the degrees indicated for the Rabbit. To enhance its intrinsic energy, display wooden carvings or sculptures of the Rabbit. Keep rabbits in pairs rather than singly.

• You can activate the same sector with any **wood element feature** since this is the intrinsic element of your animal sign. It will however be bad luck for you if this sector (i.e. East) is afflicted with a toilet or a kitchen since this would cause your personalized sector to become negatively affected.

• Because your animal sign is the Rabbit, two other sectors deemed excellent for you are those that correspond to the animal years of the Sheep and the Boar. The direction of the Sheep is South-southwest and the direction of the Boar is North-Northwest.

....

General Luck of the RABBIT in Different Years
Those born in the year of the RABBIT are advised to observe the following:

In the year 2007
It is a mixed period. Place a Cicada in the East to overcome troublemakers in your life. Also place Fu Dogs flanking your gate.

In the year 2008
Good luck. No serious problems. Place Fuk Luk Sau for good fortune luck throughout the year. Also a Laughing Buddha to bring smiles on faces.

In the year 2009
This is a difficult year. If you do not have a laughing Buddha, get an image of one to absorb all your problems.

In the year 2010
Good year for you. Hang 8 immortal coins in the East sector to bring you luck from the heavens.

In the year 2011
A dangerous period. Use windchimes in the East to dispel conflicts and to control the deadly five yellow.

In the year 2012
Rabbit people's fortunes improve. You can look forward to a year of new friendship. Wear an amethyst pendant to improve your social luck.

In the year 2013
Protect against the problems of this year by placing a red and gold laughing Buddha in the East sector. Must have crystal apple in the center of your living room.

In the year 2014
This is a year to lay low. Get yourself a wu lou and place beside your bed. The illness star is affecting you.

In the year 2015
No serious problems. You will have winning and success luck. To ensure you receive this good luck, enhance the East with a pair of dragon tortoises.

In the year 2016
The Rabbit continues to enjoy good fortune. Strengthen your luck in the South with plenty of lights and horses. This will bring you recognition luck.

In the year 2017
The Rabbit's fortunes recover. You enjoy plenty of wealth luck. Place a three-legged Pi Kan or a wealth bowl filled with ingots and jewels to further enhance prosperity luck.

In the year 2018
The Rabbit faces financial losses, possibility of robbery and theft. Must have a pair of Fu Dogs at the entrance of your main door. Carry a blue aventurine rhinoceros.

Blue Rhinoceros

The DRAGON
1916, 1928, 1940, 1952, 1964, 1976, 1988, 2000

The Dragon is the fifth sign of the Chinese Zodiac. Its intrinsic element is **earth**. The hour of the Dragon is said to be between **7.00 am to 9.00 am** in the morning. Anyone born between those hours is said to be born in the hour of the Dragon. The compass direction of the Dragon is between **97.5 degrees to 127.5 degrees**. This falls in the direction of the East-Southeast.

You will find that this sector of the house occupies an angle of 30 degrees. This sector is said to be the part of the house deemed most lucky for those residents that are born in any of the years of the Dragon, and these years are listed above. These years have not been adjusted to take account of the lunar New Year. Thus if you were born in any of the above years but during say, the month of January, chances are, you might not belong to the Dragon year but instead to the year prior to the Dragon year which is the year of the Rabbit. In the same way, you could still be a Dragon if you were born in the January of the following year. To check your date of birth against the lunar calendar, please refer to the 100-year lunar calendar at the back of the book.

To energize good wealth luck into your personal **earthly branch** sector, here are things you can do to energize the symbolism of your animal sign:

- Place images of the Dragon in the sector of your house that lies between the degrees indicated. To enhance its intrinsic energy, display dragons done in earth materials - like ceramics, porcelain, crystal and so forth. Or hang a dragon painting!

- You can activate the same sector with any **earth element feature** since this is the intrinsic element of your animal sign. It will however be bad luck for you if this sector (i.e. East-Southeast) is afflicted with a toilet or a kitchen placed there since this would cause your personalized sector to become badly affected.

- Two other sectors deemed excellent for those born in Dragon years are those that correspond to the animal years of the Monkey and the Rat. The direction of the Monkey is West-Southwest and the direction of the Rat is North.

General Luck of the DRAGON in Different Years
Those born in the year of the DRAGON are advised to observe the following:

In the year 2007
Place a dragon tortoise in the Southeast to help you get out of a bad period in your career. Light up the South for recognition luck.

In the year 2008
Good luck. No serious problems. Place Fuk Luk Sau for good fortune luck throughout the year. Also a Laughing Buddha to bring smiles on faces.

In the year 2009
This is a difficult year. If you have not got the laughing Buddha, get an image of him to quickly absorb all your problems.

In the year 2010
Good year for you. Hang a 8-immortal coins in the East sector to bring you luck from heaven.

In the year 2011
A dangerous period. Use windchimes in the East sector to dispel conflicts and to control the deadly five yellow.

In the year 2012
Dragon year people's fortunes improve. You can look forward to meeting new friends. Wear an amethyst pendant to improve your social luck.

In the year 2013
Protect against the problems of this year by placing a red and gold laughing Buddha in the East sector. Place crystal apples in the center of your living room.

In the year 2014
This is a year to stay low. Get yourself a wu lou and place beside your bed. The illness star is affecting you.

In the year 2015
No serious problems. You have winning and success luck. To ensure you receive this good luck, enhance the East sector with a pair of dragon tortoises.

Dragon Tortoise

In the year 2016
The Dragon continues with his good fortunes. Strengthen your luck by enhancing the South with plenty of lights and horses. This will bring you recognition luck.

In the year 2017
The Dragon's fortunes recover. You enjoy wealth luck this year. Place a three-legged Pi Kan or a wealth bowl filled with ingots and jewels to further enhance prosperity luck.

In the year 2018
The Dragon faces financial losses, as well as possibility of robbery and theft. Must have a pair of Fu Dogs at the entrance of your main door. Carry a blue aventurine rhinoceros.

The SNAKE
1917, 1929, 1941, 1953, 1965, 1977, 1989, 2001

The Snake is the sixth sign of the Chinese Zodiac. Its intrinsic element is **fire**. The hour of the Snake is said to be between **9.00 am to 11.00 am** in the morning. And where the Dragon is yang, the energy of the Snake is intrinsically yin. The compass direction of the Snake is between **127.5 degrees to 157.5 degrees**. This falls in the direction of the East-Southeast.

You will find that this sector of the house occupies an angle of 30 degrees. This sector is said to be the part of the house deemed most lucky for residents born in the year of the Snake. The years of the Snake are listed above. These years have not been adjusted to take account of the lunar New Year. Thus if you were born in any of the above years but during say, the month of January, chances are, you do not belong to the Snake year but instead to the year prior to the Snake year which is the year of the Dragon. In the same way, you could still be a Snake if you were born in the January of the following year. To check your date of birth against the lunar calendar, please refer to the 100-year lunar calendar at the back of the book.

To energize good wealth luck in your personal **earthly branch** sector, here are several symbolic things you might want to consider doing:

- Place images of the Snake in the sector of your house that lie between the degrees indicated above. To enhance its intrinsic energy, display the snake image in a red colour - choose images done in wood since this element produces fire!

- You can activate the same sector with any **fire element feature** since this is the intrinsic element of your animal sign. Thus keep this sector brightly lit! It will be bad luck for you if this sector (i.e. the South-southeast) is afflicted with a toilet or a kitchen placed there since this would cause your personalized sector to be badly affected.

- For those born in Snake years, sectors that correspond to the animal years of the Rooster and the Ox are also deemed excellent for them. The direction of the Rooster is West and the direction of the Ox is North-northeast.

General Luck of the SNAKE in Different Years
Those born in the year of the SNAKE are advised to observe the following:

In the year 2007
Display a Pi Yao facing Northwest to overcome the conflict with Grand Duke Jupiter. Get a dragon tortoise with ru yi and place in the Southeast to give you good career luck.

In the year 2008
Career luck needs a boost. Create a water feature for the North and display a 3 legged Pi Kan near the front of the door.

In the year 2009
Fantastic year. Display a wish fulfilling jewel in the Southeast to make your wishes come true. Place a water feature here too.

In the year 2010
The Snake requires protection luck this year. Place a pair of elephants by the main door and display a blue rhinoceros inside the home.

In the year 2011
A good year when energizing the Southeast with a money plant hanging with coins. Snake will enjoy good unexpected windfall luck.

In the year 2012
A bad year for the Snake. Control the Southeast with a 5 element pagoda to protect you against accidents, loss of money and loss of relationships.

In the year 2013
Powerful friends bring opportunities and good fortune. Place crystals in the Southwest. Display the Fuk Luk Sau in the Northwest.

In the year 2014
A tiring year. Activate the luck of the center with an amethyst tree and place your friends and allies in your animal sign direction.

In the year 2015
It is good for you to travel overseas this year. Wear a longevity symbol pendant to overcome health worries and sickness.

In the year 2016
A year of career enhancement. The Snake's career luck is poised for growth. Place a dragon tortoise in the Southeast to activate career luck.

In the year 2017
Keep an arowana in the East sector of your living room for money luck and to protect against loss of money.

In the year 2018
Display a wealth god in the Southeast sector of the home. This will bring you plenty of prosperity luck to your house.

5 Element Pagoda

The HORSE
1918, 1930, 1942, 1954, 1966, 1978, 1990, 2002

The Horse is the seventh sign of the Chinese Zodiac. Its intrinsic element is **fire.** The hour of the Horse is said to be between **11.00 am to 1.00 pm** in the morning. Anyone born between those hours is said to be born in the hour of the Horse. The compass direction of the Horse is between **157.5 degrees to 187.5 degrees.** This falls in the direction of the South.

You will find that this sector of the house occupies an angle of 30 degrees. This sector is said to be the part of the house deemed most lucky for those residents who are born in any of the years of the Horse. The years of the Horse are listed above. These years have not been adjusted to take account of the lunar New Year. Thus if you were born in any of the above years but during say, the month of January, chances are, you do not belong to the Horse year but instead to the year prior to the Horse year, which is the year of the Snake. In the same way, you could still be a Horse if you were born in the January of the following year. To check your date of birth against the lunar calendar, please refer to the 100-year lunar calendar at the back of the book.

To energize good wealth luck in your personal **earthly branch** sector, here are several symbolic things you can do:

- Place images of the Horse in the sector of your house that lies between the degrees indicated above. To enhance its intrinsic energy, display the horse image in whites and reds ie yang colours - choose images done in wood since this element produces fire!

- You can activate the same sector with any **fire element feature** since this is the intrinsic element of your animal sign. Thus keep this sector brightly lit! It will be bad luck for you if this sector (i.e. the South) is where a toilet or the kitchen is located since this would cause your personalized sector to be seriously afflicted.

- For those born in Horse years, sectors that correspond to the animal years of the Dog and the Tiger are also deemed excellent. The direction of the Dog is West-Northwest and the direction of the Tiger is East-Northeast.

General Luck of the HORSE in Different Years
Those born in the year of the HORSE are advised to observe the following:

In the year 2007
A year of unexpected windfall luck! Display an 8-immortal set by your entrance door. Having big parties in your house as frequently as possible.

In the year 2008
Financial problems and bad luck in money matters. Display a camel to overcome your financial difficulties.

In the year 2009
Place a Rabbit in the East sector to activate romance luck. Also have the 4 scholastic objects in the South if you are still studying.

In the year 2010
Bad year for romance. Display 6 smooth crystal balls in the South to overcome bad energy and guard against misunderstandings.

In the year 2011
This year the Horse needs to be extra careful with health. Do more exercise and take healthy foods. Carry a jade wu lou with you.

In the year 2012
Place a 3 legged toad for continued money luck in your job. Remove all the unwanted items from the South sector. Make it as clean as possible in this area.

In the year 2013
Travel luck is good. Place a pair of precious elephants near the front door and carry a conch shell with you to bring good travel luck.

In the year 2014
A fantastic year for Horse! Full of money and wealth luck. Grab opportunities you get to start your own business or start new job.

In the year 2015
A moderate year. Display a pair of blue rhinoceros in the South to control the violent star. Take care of your wallet and money!

In the year 2016
A year of unexpected difficulties and obstacles. Display the 8 immortals sitting on the dragon by your entrance door.

In the year 2017
Financial problems and money losses. Display a 5 element pagoda in the South for protection. Avoid high risk investments.

In the year 2018
Good year to meet up with friends and to really get to know your old pals. Display an amethyst tree in the Southwest to strengthen friendship luck.

3-Legged Toad

⽺ The SHEEP
1919, 1931, 1943, 1955, 1967, 1979, 1991, 2003

The Sheep is the eighth sign of the Chinese Zodiac. Its intrinsic element is **earth.** The hour of the Sheep is said to be between **1.00 pm to 3.00 pm** in the afternoon. Anyone born between those hours is said to be born in the hour of the Sheep. The compass direction of the Sheep is between **187.5 degrees to 217.5 degrees.** This falls in the direction of the South-Southwest.

You will find that this sector of the house occupies an angle of 30 degrees. This sector is said to be the part of the house deemed most lucky for those residents who are born in any of the years of the Sheep. The years of the Sheep are listed above. These years have not been adjusted to take account of the lunar New Year. Thus if you were born in any of the above years but say in the month of January, chances are, you might not belong to the Sheep year but instead to the year prior to the Sheep year which is the year

of the Horse. In the same way, you could still be a Sheep year person if you were born in the January of the following year. To check your date of birth against the lunar calendar, please refer to the 100-year lunar calendar at the back of the book.

To energize good wealth luck into your personal **earthly branch** sector, here are several symbolic things you can do:

....

• Place images of the Sheep or Goat in the sector of your house that lies between the degrees indicated for the Sheep. To enhance its intrinsic energy display the sheep image in **earth element** materials!

• You can also activate the same sector with the fire element, since fire produces earth. The sector will also benefit from porcelain and other decorative ceramic ware.

• For those born in Sheep years, there are two other sectors that are also deemed most excellent. These are sectors that correspond to the animal years of the Boar and the Rabbit. The sector which is identified with the Boar is North-Northwest and the sector of the Rabbit is the East.

....

General Luck of the SHEEP in Different Years
Those born in the year of the SHEEP are advised to observe the following:

In the year 2007
Place a gold laughing Buddha sitting on an emperor chair in the Northwest to absorb problems that come your way this year.

In the year 2008
A year of money loss. Money luck comes easily but also goes out easily. Place a lock coin under your pillow to help you.

In the year 2009
Money luck is great. Place 6 metal coins in the Southwest to bring heaven luck from the heavens.

In the year 2010
Misfortune luck hits you this year. Place a Kwan Kung near the front door to ward off bad energy.

In the year 2011
A serene year when money luck improves considerably. Place coins and the gold bars anywhere in the living room to symbolize the house full of jade.

In the year 2012
A period to socialize with people. However, do not argue and find fault in people. You will end up in the losing end. Carry a peach aventurine apple to calm down the bad energy.

In the year 2013
A good time for you to relax and lay down. Take care of your health and go for medical check up regularly. Hang the metal windchime wu lou to help you.

In the year 2014
Good news! There is an improvement on your career luck. You may get promoted or increment. To make your wishes succeed, wear the mantra ring.

In the year 2015
A year of minor setback. Carry a 12 horoscopes amulet coin to help you boost your good luck to the maximum and overcome the minor setback.

In the year 2016
The Sheep's confidence returns in this auspicious year. Place the wish fulfilling cow in the living room and install a water feature in the southwest.

In the year 2017
A sobering period. The presence of the rhinoceros or elephant will be great help. It is good time to invite a laughing Buddha.

In the year 2018
This is a good year for you to go all out for investment. Heaven luck is assisting you. Carry 6 gold coins with you.

Laughing Buddha

猴 The MONKEY
1920, 1932, 1944, 1956, 1968, 1980, 1992, 2004

The Monkey is the ninth sign of the Chinese Zodiac. Its intrinsic element is **metal.** The hour of the Monkey is said to be between **3.00 pm to 5.00 pm** in the late afternoon. Anyone born between those hours is said to be born in the hour of the Monkey. The compass direction of the Monkey is between **217.5 degrees to 247.5 degrees.** This falls in the direction of the West-Southwest.

You will find that this sector of the house occupies an angle of 30 degrees. This sector is said to be the part of the house deemed most lucky for those residents who are born in the year of the Monkey. The years of the Monkey are listed above. These years have not been adjusted to take account of the lunar New Year. Thus if you were born in any of the above years but during say, the month of January, chances are, you might not belong to the Monkey year but instead to the year prior to the Monkey year which is the year of the Sheep. In the same way, you could still be a Monkey year person if you were born in the January of the following year. To check your date of birth against the lunar calendar, please refer to the 100-year lunar calendar at the back of the book.

To energize good wealth luck in your personal **earthly branch** sector, here are several symbolic things you can do:

* Place images of the Monkey in the sector of your house that lies between the degrees indicated for the Monkey. To enhance its intrinsic energy, display the auspicious painting of *monkey with peaches.* This scene is also painted onto ceramics or porcelain.

* You can activate the same sector with any **metal element** feature, since this is the intrinsic element of your animal sign. Thus bells and windchimes are suitable for this sector. It will be bad luck for you if a toilet or the kitchen is located in this sector (i.e. the West-Southwest) since this would cause your personalized sector to be badly affected.

* Those born in Monkey years will also benefit from good fortune symbols placed in sectors that correspond to Rat and Dragon years. The sector of the Rat is North and that of the Dragon is East-Southeast.

General Luck of the MONKEY in Different Years
Those born in the year of the MONKEY are advised to observe the following:

In the year 2007
You need a Tai Sui coin to protect you against the Grand Duke Jupiter this year. Make sure you have the Pi Yao in the Northwest of your house.

In the year 2008
The violent and robbery star has flown into your palace. This brings loss of money and risk of being cheated by someone. Carry a blue rhinoceros with you at all times.

In the year 2009
Display good fortune symbols to enhance this moderate year. Place a water feature in the Southeast to activate for money luck.

In the year 2010
An unpredictable and uncertain time. The Monkey will benefit from placing a snake with coins to improve money-making opportunities.

In the year 2011
Display a God of Wealth in the Northwest. Place a Ru Yi on your desk. Energize the Southeast with water. Then your luck will be much improved.

In the year 2012
This is a good time to travel overseas and relax your mind. Enhance travel luck with a conch sheel in your living room. Wear an Om syllable pendant to protect you.

In the year 2013
A year of sickness for Monkey. Place a longevity god in the East sector to promote good health and carry a golden Wu Lou to protect against sickness.

In the year 2014
A year of good luck when helpful people enhance your good fortune. Place your allies and secret friends in the Southwest to bring you mentor luck.

In the year 2015
A year when you will get noticed by someone. Enhance the South sector with lots of light to ensure a continuity of overall fame and recognition luck.

In the year 2016
A year of excellent gains. Place a gem tree in the Southwest to crystallize your good fortune luck and bring moneymaking opportunities.

Gem Tree

In the year 2017
A year when it is best to be cautious. Place a pair of elephants with trunk up by the entrance. A pair of chi lin at your working desk will enhance career luck.

In the year 2018
A year when fortunes improve considerably. Hang six gold coins in the Southwest to bring heaven luck and unexpected bonuses.

The ROOSTER
1921, 1933, 1945, 1957, 1969, 1981, 1993, 2005

The Rooster is the tenth sign of the Chinese Zodiac. Its intrinsic element is **metal.** The hour of the Rooster is said to be between **5.00 pm to 7.00 pm** in the late afternoon. Anyone born between those hours is said to be born in the hour of the Rooster. The compass direction of the Rooster is between **247.5 degrees to 277.5 degrees.** This falls in the direction of the West.

You will find that this sector of the house occupies an angle of 30 degrees. This sector is said to be the part of the house deemed most lucky for residents born in the year of the Rooster. The years of the Rooster are listed above. These years have not been adjusted to take account of the lunar New Year. Thus if you were born in any of the above years but during say, the month of January, chances are, you do not belong to the Rooster year but instead to the year prior to the Rooster year which is the year of the Monkey. In the same way, you could still be a Rooster if you were born in the January of the following year. To check your date of birth against the lunar calendar, please refer to the 100-year lunar calendar at the back of the book.

To energize good wealth luck in your personal **earthly branch** sector, here are several symbolic things you can apply:

....

* Place images of the Rooster in the sector of your house that falls between the degrees indicated for the Rooster. To enhance its intrinsic energy, display Rooster images and sculptures made of ceramics or porcelain.

* You can activate the sector with the **metal element** since this is the intrinsic element of your animal sign. Thus bells and windchimes are fine for this sector. It will be bad luck for you if this sector (i.e. the West) is afflicted with a toilet or a kitchen placed here since this would cause your personalized sector to be badly affected.

* Rooster year people also benefit from sectors that correspond to the animal years of the Snake and the Ox. The direction of the Snake is South-Southeast and the direction of the Ox is North-Northeast.

....

General Luck of the ROOSTER in Different Years
Those born in the year of the ROOSTER are advised to observe the following:

In the year 2007
Energize the luck of the SW by placing crystals and crystal balls here. Place a chi lin in the house for protection against betrayal.

In the year 2008
There will be money and health problems this year. Place a red triangle crystal and a longevity god in the living room.

In the year 2009
A good year when finances will improve. Place prosperity and wealth symbols in the living room. Make sure you take care of your health.

In the year 2010
A great deal of money and career luck this year. Enhance by displaying the god of wealth sitting on a tiger in the office.

In the year 2011
The Rooster is said to be afflicted by the presence of Grand Duke Jupiter in the East. Place a Pi Yao facing East to overcome the Grand Duke.

Pi Yao

In the year 2012
An excellent period which benefits from the wealth vase and the gem tree. Other excellent enhancers are the 3 legged Pi Kan flanking the main door.

In the year 2013
Financial problems this year can be reduced with the presence of the dragon tortoise and fu dogs. Avoid taking any high risk investment.

In the year 2014
Very good mentor luck this year although money fortunes are mediocre. Energize the NW with 8 rod metal windchime.

In the year 2015
A difficult year for Roosters when plans go awry and love life gets seriously afflicted. Place a gold laughing Buddha to help dissolve problems.

In the year 2016
There will be plenty of opportunities for you to meet new people. Attend all the invited parties and you will meet your partner or new friend.

In the year 2017
A year when you need to stay focus on your work and avoid any argument. This helps to avoid any misunderstand and disagreement.

In the year 2018
The Rooster is in health problem. Avoid staying out late and burn midnight oil. Take a nap when you feel tired and exhausted.

The DOG
1922, 1934, 1946, 1958, 1970, 1982, 1994, 2006

The Dog is the eleventh sign of the Chinese zodiac. Its intrinsic element is **earth**. The hour of the Dog is said to be between **7.00 pm to 9.00 pm** in the evening. Anyone born between those hours is said to be born in the hour of the Dog. The compass direction of the Dog is between **277.5 degrees to 307.5 degrees**. This falls in the direction of the West-Northwest.

You will find that this sector of the house occupies an angle of 30 degrees. This sector is said to be the part of the house deemed most lucky for those residents who are born in the year of the Dog. The years of the Dog are listed above. These years have not been adjusted to take account of the lunar New Year. Thus if you were born in any of the above years but during say, the month of January, chances are, you do not belong to the Dog year but instead to the year prior to the Dog year which is the year of the Rooster. In the same way you, could still be a Dog if you were born in the January of the following year. To check your date of birth against the lunar calendar, please refer to the 100-year lunar calendar at the back of the book.

To energize good wealth luck in your personal **earthly branch** sector, here are several symbolic things you can apply:

- Place images of the Dog in the sector of your house that falls between the degrees indicated for the Dog. To enhance its intrinsic energy display Dog images and sculptures that are made of ceramics or porcelain. This enhances the **earth element**.

- You can activate the sector with other objects that suggest the earth element since this is the intrinsic element of your animal sign. It will be bad luck for you if a toilet or the kitchen is placed here (i.e. the West-Northwest) since this would seriously afflict your sector.

- Dog year people also benefit from sectors that correspond to the animal years of the Tiger and the Horse. The direction of the Tiger is East-Northeast and the direction of the Horse is South.

General Luck of the DOG in Different Years
Those born in the year of the DOG are advised to observe the following:

In the year 2007
A quiet period when you benefit from the presence of the Ksiddigarbha monk. It is best that this monk is a figurine.

In the year 2008
A year full of illness and sickness. Display an 8 immortal Wu Lou and wear a longevity symbol to overcome the bad chi.

In the year 2009
Place a dragon in the Northwest to ensure your career continues to sail upward and is at least stable. Try not to get entangled in disputes.

In the year 2010
For luck, place crystals along the Northwest walls of the house to capture yang energy from sunlight.

In the year 2011
A year of expansion and money luck. Magnify good fortune with kwan kung and a small water feature in the Northwest. Career luck is good.

In the year 2012
Small setbacks this year, but these can be nullified by placing a blue rhinoceros with double horns in the Northwest as this will control the robbery star.

In the year 2013
A smooth year. Harmony can be maintained by placing 6 smooth crystal balls in the center of the living room.

In the year 2014
A tiresome year when things go wrong. Place 5 element pagoda for protection against loss of face and money.

In the year 2015
Good year for education luck. Place the 4 scholastic objects in the Northwest to enhance study luck. You will do well in exams.

In the year 2016
The Dog will suffer some minor setbacks with work and family. You will find yourself easily upset and angry. Place a crystal apple on your work desk to control your emotions.

In the year 2017
Health setbacks make this an unhappy and tired year. Dissipate this by placing a gold laughing Buddha in the living room and a Wu Lou next to your bed.

In the year 2018
Fortunes and success luck will increase to a greater height. Place a jumping carp in the North sector of your home to empower your luck.

6 Smooth Crystal Balls

The BOAR
1923, 1935, 1947, 1959, 1971, 1983, 1995, 2007

The Boar is the twelfth sign of the Chinese Zodiac. Its intrinsic element is **Water.** The hour of the Boar is said to be between **9.00 PM to 11.00PM** in the night. Anyone born between those hours is said to be born in the hour of the Boar. The compass direction of the boar is between **307.5 degrees to 337.5 degrees.** This falls in the direction of the North-Northwest.

You will find that this sector of the house occupies an angle of 30 degrees. This sector is said to be part of the house deemed most lucky for those residents who are born in any of the years of the boar. The years of the boar are listed above. These years have not been adjusted to take into account of the lunar New Year. Thus if you were born in any of the above years but during say, the month of January, chances are, you do not belong to the Boar year but instead to the year prior to the Boar year which is the year of the Dog. In the same way,

you could still be a boar if you were born in the January of the following year. To check your date of birth against the lunar calendar, please refer to 100 year lunar calendar at the back of the book.

To energize good wealth luck in your personal **earthly branch** sector, here are several symbolic things you can apply.

....

- Place images of the Boar in the sector of your house that falls between the degrees indicated above (North–Northwest, 307.5 degrees to 337.5 degrees). To enhance its intrinsic energy, display Boar Images next to water. This enhances the water element of this animal sign.

- You can activate the sector with **water features** like aquarium and ponds since water is the intrinsic element of your animal sign. It will be bad luck for you if a toilet or kitchen is located here (i.e. the West-Northwest) since this would seriously afflict your sector.

- Boar year people also benefit from sectors that correspond to the animal years of the Sheep and the Rabbit. The direction of the Sheep is South–Southwest and the direction of the Rabbit is East.

....

General Luck of the BOAR in Different Years
Those born in the year of the BOAR are advised to observe the following:

In the year 2007
A mixed year. Place a ksiddigarbha staff in the Northwest to control the conflict energy. Enhance the Southwest with water.

In the year 2008
A moderate year when the Boar will benefit from the mongoose being displayed in the living room.

In the year 2009
There is plenty of money luck, but love relationships are difficult. Place a pair of mandarin ducks in the bedroom.

In the year 2010
You need the flying horse to bring you good recognition and fame luck. Place a mountain painting on the wall behind your office chair to receive support from bosses.

In the year 2011
An excellent year when fortunes rebound. Place a pot of gold in the Northwest to bring benefits and create the money luck you need.

In the year 2012
Not a good year. Some financial setbacks. Place door guardians at your entrance door. Also carry a blue aventurine rhinoceros.

In the year 2013
You will need all prosperity enhancers this period to give your money luck a boost. Display a money tree in your living room and try your hand at making a wealth vase.

In the year 2014
A bad year. The best thing you can do is to invite in the Fuk Luk Sau if you have not already done so. Carry a 5 element pagoda keychain with you to avert bad luck.

In the year 2015
The Boar enjoys romance luck, which can be enhanced by placing a pair of mandarin ducks in the bedroom. This is a good year for Boars who are still studying.

In the year 2016
The Boar has to deal with gossip and troublemakers. There could be setbacks on the romance front. Place a triangular red crystal in the Northwest.

In the year 2017
Old Boars needs to be careful with their health. Take more healthy foods and have enough sleep. Do some light exercise and carry a jade wu lou with you.

In the year 2018
A smooth and happy year that is excellent for your career and relationships. You will benefit from a horse in the South.

Flying Painted Pony

Chapter Eleven:
Yin & Yang and Lucky Hexagrams

Feng shui is about harmony brought about by the perfect balancing of yin and yang energy. The sun is yang and the moon is yin. Dark and cold, noise and quiet and darkness and brightness should be used in a clever way to symbolize balance. When the effect is further enhanced by the presence of at least one of the three auspicious hexagrams - chien, kun and sheng - the feng shui of any space is usually considerably improved.

> Yin and Yang are primordial forces that are opposites.
> YIN is dark. YANG is bright. YIN is passive. YANG is active.

YIN is female. YANG is male. But Yin and Yang are complementary, not opposing forces. Yin Yang is pictorially represented by the universally known symbol shown above which depicts an egg showing the yolk and the white strongly differentiated, the black and white colours distinguishing the two principles.

YANG symbolizes heaven, the Sun, Light, Vigour, Positive energy. Yang is the dragon, male, strong, hard, fiery, hot, warm. In Feng Shui, mountains and landforms represent Yang energy.

YIN symbolizes the earth, the moon, darkness, female and governs the cold and soft; the deadly, the negative. Yin is the Tiger. In feng shui valleys and waters usually possess Yin attributes.

The Hexagrams come from a total of 64 six lined symbols that make up the I Ching - the Book of Changes. The I Ching, China's most important book, goes back to mythical antiquity. Nearly all that is great and significant in the cultural history of China can be traced to the I Ching, which is also a book of divination. The three lucky hexagrams highlighted in this chapter - *chien*, *kun* and sheng are the three luckiest hexagrams of the I Ching. In themselves, they are good fortune symbols that bring auspicious luck to households.

The moon is a powerful symbol and source of yin energy

In the practice of feng shui, both yin and yang energies must balance at an optimum level to create good vibrations for the home. In the houses of the living, yang energies are considered most precious and vital, but never to the extent that yin energy becomes absent. Also, bedrooms and other rooms which are meant for rest and relaxation would benefit from fresh yin energy. The moon and moonlight is generally associated with yin energy that is clear and auspicious. This is the kind of yin energy that is auspicious, not the stale, stagnant kind associated with the dead and dying. Thus, while we do not want yin energy generated by dying plants, for instance, we would welcome the pure yin energies of a full moon.

There are many legends associated with the moon, of which probably the most enticing is that the moon is the paradise abode of the God of Marriage. It is believed that the man on the moon is the God of Marriage, and young maidens wanting to contract a good match should use moon energy to help energize their love corner. There are special Taoist rituals that involve the use of moon energy said to be most effective in helping young maidens find true love. Alas, I do not know these rituals, otherwise I would happily pass them on to those of you who might wish to use them.

- I do know that you can bathe in water that has been energized by the moon. This will attract a better love life for maidens. Place a pail of water out on a full moon night, making sure it reflects the rays of the moon. From this water, make a *moon bath*. Add seven types of flowers, two types of scents and soak in the moon energy.

- The moon is also associated with the hare or **rabbit**, as well as the very auspicious **3 legged toad,** whose spirit is supposedly residing on the moon. The 3 legged toad, or *Chan Chu* in Chinese, was once the wife of one of the Eight Immortals who stole the elixir of Immortality from her husband for which crime she was supposedly turned into a toad by the God of Heaven and banished to live in the moon!

The sun is a powerful symbol and source of yang energy

One of the easiest ways of capturing yang energy is to ensure that the inside of homes gets an occasional bath of sunshine. This is because the sun is the most potent symbol and source of yang energy. The sun purifies and energizes at the same time. For this reason, homes that suffer from insufficient sunshine are said to be excessively yin - a state that spells a surfeit of inauspicious energy. This sort of situation is usually caused by overgrown trees that totally block out the sunlight. Trees that surround any home should always be trimmed back regularly so that the precious sunlight shines through. There are several methods of harnessing the sun's precious yang energy to enhance your overall feng shui.

- Firstly, you can use **yang energized water** to supplement all the water used for watering plants, to supplement

ponds and aquariums and for filling vases for flowers. Place a pail of water out in the sun and let the water stand in direct sunlight for at least three hours. The best sunshine is morning sunshine. Remember that sun energized water is full of life!

- Secondly, you can hang **faceted lead crystal** along a window to catch the direct sunlight shining along any wall. The crystal will break up the sunlight and create lots of beautiful rainbows in your home. This will bathe your home with precious yang energy that creates harmony and a feeling of optimism for the home. I hang these small crystals on many of my windows all over my home and thus have **rainbows** almost daily.

- Thirdly, you can refresh sunshine energies in your home on a regular basis by throwing open all the doors and windows and drawing all the curtains and blinds so that sunlight pours into the home. This cleanses all stagnant and stale yin energies which may have gathered and accumulated. I recommend you do this once a month.

The most powerful hexagram is *Chien - the Creative*

乾

CHIEN

Chien is the first of the 64 hexagrams of the I Ching. It is the ultimate symbol of yang energy. It comprises six solid, unbroken lines. Chien creates light giving, active and spirited chi, which attracts great good fortune. Chien is also said to bring luck from heaven whose essence is power.

Chien benefits the Patriarch of the family, the leader or breadwinner. It is best placed in the Northwest of the house or living room. This is indicated by the Later Heaven Arrangement of the trigrams around the Pa Kua symbol. By placing images of the Chien hexagram in the Northwest, the luck of sublime success is created. This will be fueled by the full power of heaven therefore implying great strength. The capacity represented by the hexagram Chien is creative, and it is at its zenith during the summer months when the full benefits will be felt.

The best way to simulate this hexagram is to incorporate it into the design of seams and lines on ceilings, walls and furniture. If you find it difficult to incorporate 6 lines, you can also try using 3 lines because this is often sufficient for activating the Chien symbol.

If your main door is located in the NW sector of your home, or it is directly facing the NW direction, it is a good idea to "carve" or emboss the image of Chien onto the door.

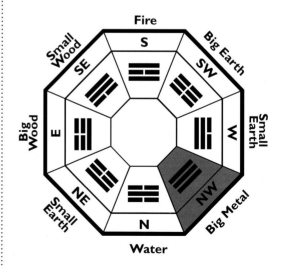

This benefits the feng shui of the whole house, but in particular, it benefits the feng shui of the breadwinner. Meanwhile, if the main bedroom is located in the NW sector of the house, incorporating solid lines onto ceiling and wall cornices activates the Chien energy.

The hexagram of the matriarch is *Kun - the Receptive*

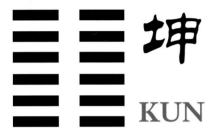

KUN

Kun encapsulates all of earth energy. Thus, where Chien is heaven, Kun signifies the earth; and where Chien is the Patriarch, Kun manifests the essence of the Matriarch. This hexagram stands for the ultimate yin energy. It is female where Chien is male; and it is made up of six broken lines where Chien was made up of six unbroken lines.

The place of Kun is the Southwest, as indicated in the Yang Pa Kua arrangement of trigrams. Its element is big earth. Thus Kun benefits in the form of powerful earth energy. Activating this hexagram will benefit the females of the family, and in particular the matriarch or dowager of the household. It is an especially excellent enhancer for widows who have to transform themselves into the family breadwinner.

Activate Kun by incorporating the symbol of broken lines into furniture and wall designs in the sector of the Southwest. When you complement this with other earth energizers in this sector the luck created is most auspicious. The hexagram brings sublime success, usually brought about through the perseverance of the mother. It ensures a smooth progress of all projects undertaken by the matriarch.

Energizing the Kun hexagram is also extremely beneficial for relationship luck. Friends can be found from all the eight directions and especially from all the four cardinal directions of the compass. These will be friends you can count on. Those wishing for luck associated with matters of the heart can energize the SW with images of the Kun hexagram. Carve the symbol onto a table in the SW, and then shine a bright light on it. Combining the fire element with that of Kun creates a wonderful balance of yin and yang and also enhances the earth element, since fire produces earth.

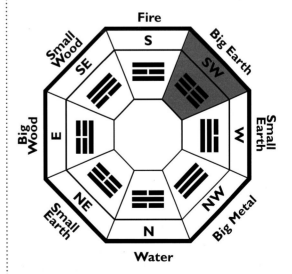

Feng shui recommends the hexagram *Sheng* - to grow upwards

This is hexagram number 46 - the hexagram SHENG, which is made up of the trigrams *Sun* below and *Kun* above. The image above is of wood inside the earth pushing upwards, and the meaning is the attainment of a state of steady growth. It is a very auspicious hexagram, as it implies inevitable and supreme success. It also implies that one career path, as well as one's path through life, will be relatively free of obstacles. There are no hindrances to achieving one aspirations. The image is illustrated here. The trigram Sun is the wood below the ground. It pushes upward and grows into a large tree. The metaphor brings good fortune, and is expressed in the I Ching this way:

> Within the earth, wood grows
> The image of pushing upward
> Thus the superior man of good character
> Heaps up small things
> To achieve something high and great.

Copy this hexagram and place it in the East or Southeast - the sectors of the wood element, to harness the luck of this hexagram. If your main entrance door is located in either of these wood sectors, it will be most beneficial to incorporate the hexagram into a door design. You can also draw out the hexagram and place it above the doorway just inside the house.

SHENG implies that in the early stages of growth initial impetus comes from one's own confidence. Yet because it is early days the hexagram also advises humility. Then only will help come from all quarters.

SHENG also implies obtaining the help and support of powerful patrons who notice your perseverance and hard work. In other words, you will also enjoy the luck of being recognized for your hard work by someone who can help you. This mentor luck continues as long as one is steady, and continues to persevere. Because of the various layers of luck offered by the meaning of Sheng, practitioners of the I Ching school of feng shui highly recommend placing this hexagram as a good luck symbol.

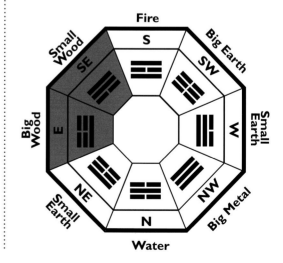

Chapter Twelve:
Auspicious Deities

The deities featured in this chapter are extremely popular, and I recommend them not for any esoteric reasons but for the symbolism of auspiciousness and happiness they each represent.

There are **Gods of Wealth** as well as the ever popular Three Star Gods **Fuk Luk Sau**. Another immensely popular deity is the **Laughing Buddha** who carries a huge bag to scoop up all your troubles and problems. Place these deities in your home to signify plenty of happiness and abundance, and also for protection, but please do so only if they do not offend your religious sensitivities.

Tsai Shen Yeh the powerful god of wealth

Tsai Shen Yeh

This powerful God of wealth is usually depicted seated on a Tiger. He is dressed in dragon robes. In his right hand he carries a symbolic ingot of gold as well as a bundle of coins tied together with red thread. Cradled in his left arm is a staff with all the precious symbols. His expression is fierce but relaxed.

If you wish to invite Tsai Shen Yeh into your home, make sure you have prepared a prominent place for him to sit. He should always face the front door, but not necessarily directly, although if he does face the door directly it is perfectly acceptable. He can be placed at the corner of the living room or foyer that is diagonal to the main door, and he should be placed on a table. Tsai Shen Yeh should never be placed on the floor.

If you have Buddhist altars in your home where you pray to Buddha or the Goddess of Mercy, or any altars of other religions, please do not place **Tsai Shen Yeh** on the same altar. This would deem to be most disrespectful to the Deities that you do pray to. I have been advised by people I respect highly that it is not necessary to worship the God of Wealth. However, we can make symbolic offerings to him, the best of which are to be fresh oranges. Placing a bowl of oranges with some red paper is supposed to be ritually auspicious.

Never place images like the God of Wealth in your bedroom, as this is said to be very inauspicious. You may if you wish place him in the dining room, but the best place is the living room. You may place the God of Wealth in the corner of the living room that corresponds to your most auspicious direction under the KUA formula or based on your animal year of birth. These lucky sectors are based on two separate schools of feng shui and you can decide which school you wish to follow. There is no necessity to be confused. Feng shui is a science with great breadth of interpretations, so my suggestion is to do what works for you!

Tua Peh Kong the hokkien god of wealth

Tua Peh Kong

This is the Hokkien God of Wealth and he is worshipped as a Taoist deity of wealth. His image is different from the previously presented God of Wealth. Here **Tua Peh Kong** is depicted standing and dressed in robes that feature auspicious symbols and holding a banner proclaiming your wealth has arrived in his right hand. In his left hand is the **Ru Yi** - the symbol of authority, a most auspicious symbol. A jade Ru Yi is believed to confer fabulous luck for those who want power and authority. The Ru Yi is thus an auspicious symbol in its own right. Here, the God of Wealth is carrying it to emphasize the great good fortune which the God can bestow upon those who ask him for wealth and success.

This Deity is revered by the Hokkiens and in the Penang area where there are many small shrines set up by those who have benefited from his largesse. I am also told that there is a big temple devoted to him in the Chinatown area of Kuala Lumpur set up by those who have benefited from praying to him.

The Ru Yi - an auspicious symbol of power and authority. Display in the North of your living room for career luck.

There are two other Gods of Wealth and these are the military and civilian aspects of the same deity, said to be the deified image of a former sage known as Pi Kan who lived during the 12th century.

The Three Star Gods Fuk Luk Sau

The Three Star Gods are the popular Deities of Wealth, Health and Longevity, also known as Fuk Luk Sau. Their images are eagerly sought after, and only the Laughing Buddha matches their popularity in Chinese households.

These Star Gods are often mistaken for the Three Pure Beings of the Taoist trinity which comprise the Jade Ruler of Heaven. It is important not to make this mistake.

The Laughing Buddha is also known as the Fat Buddha, the Buddha of Wealth, and the Buddha of Happiness

The Laughing Buddha is one of the most beloved of Buddha images. His laughing form can be seen in Chinese homes and Chinese restaurants throughout the world. He has been referred to as the Buddha of Wealth because his image is believed to bring prosperity luck to those engaged in any kind of business. Those who consider him the Buddha of Wealth assume that his big bag contains lots of gold ingots and precious gemstones. Some also maintain that all his wealth is carried in his big round tummy, and that the bigger the tummy, the more auspicious the image! To enjoy the Buddha's blessings, one should stroke the big belly each day.

Fuk Luk Sau is best placed in the dining area of the house. Many families have several sets, placing them both at home and in the office of the breadwinner. Personally, I have three sets of Fuk Luk Sau. I have one set in my family dining room, one set in my family TV room and one set in my living room. This is because the meanings associated with these Three Star Gods are simply so auspicious.

Basically, they signify overall good luck. They bring harmony to the home and they overcome negative vibes. They also bring good health, lots of prosperity and plenty of descendants luck and this is indicated by one of the Three Star Gods carrying a child.

The picture above gives a clearer view of the Three Star Gods, placed in their usual position with the God of Longevity, *Sau*, wearing robes that have the longevity symbol and carrying the nectar of immortality in his bottle gourd. **Fuk** carries a Ru Yi to signify power, success and authority, while **Luk** carries a child to signify descendants luck.

Others say that the Laughing Buddha is the Buddha of Happiness because he is said to simply love scooping up all the unhappiness, problems and worries of human beings and stuffing them all inside his big bag. Nothing makes him happier than transforming problems into happiness. And because all of mankind has so many problems, his bag is said to be big and heavy. This is also the reason why he is shown laughing happily - because he is able to pick up what he loves most - other people's problems and unhappiness! I love this version of the story because it seems very authentic and is in accordance with Buddha's teachings.

In reality the Laughing Buddha is the Maitreya Buddha, the Buddha to come

Maitreya Buddha

The Laughing Buddha is regarded by many Chinese Buddhists as the future Buddha to come - also called the Maitreya Buddha. Only of course all other representations of the Maitreya Buddha from other cultures show a most handsome and striking image. Most of the images of Maitreya are completely unlike the Chinese version. I went looking for the story of why the Chinese Maitreya, which has become so popular as an auspicious symbol, looks so fat and oversized, and discovered

a most novel explanation. The story goes that because Buddha Maitreya in one of his lifetimes was so handsome that many young maidens swooned over him, in his compassion, Maitreya decided to manifest in a fat and oversized form, since this would ensure none of that.

Hence the Chinese version of Maitreya is fat and laughing. In Chinese, this Buddha is known as **Mi Lo Foh** - literally Laughing Buddha. Place the image of this Buddha in the living room, preferably directly facing the front door and as large as possible. You can select any posture you wish. The Laughing Buddha is sculptured into many forms and using many materials, from ceramics to ivory to cloisonné and wood. You might want to look for a medium that corresponds to the element deemed most auspicious for you. There are many beautiful versions of this most auspicious image, so do take your time selecting one that particularly appeals to you.

> When you buy an image of Laughing Buddha, look out for his smile, his big tummy and the bag he carries. These are the 3 main symbols that you must like - then you are said to have an affinity with the image who will then bring you loads of luck.

The Hundred Year Lunar Calendar

ANIMAL	CHINESE NEW YEAR DATES		EARTHLY BRANCH	HEAVENLY STEM
Rat (Water)	FEB 5, 1924	- JAN 23, 1925	WATER	WOOD
Ox (Earth)	JAN 24, 1925	- FEB 12, 1926	EARTH	WOOD
Tiger (Wood)	FEB 13, 1926	- FEB 1, 1927	WOOD	FIRE
Rabbit (Wood)	FEB 2, 1927	- JAN 22, 1928	WOOD	FIRE
Dragon (Earth)	JAN 23, 1928	- FEB 9, 1929	EARTH	EARTH
Snake (Fire)	FEB 10, 1929	- JAN 29, 1930	FIRE	EARTH
Horse (Fire)	JAN 30, 1930	- FEB 16, 1931	FIRE	METAL
Sheep (Earth)	FEB 17, 1931	- FEB 5, 1932	EARTH	METAL
Monkey (Metal)	FEB 6, 1932	- JAN 25, 1933	METAL	WATER
Rooster (Metal)	JAN 26, 1933	- FEB 13, 1934	METAL	WATER
Dog (Earth)	FEB 14, 1934	- FEB 3, 1935	EARTH	WOOD
Boar (Water)	FEB 4, 1935	- JAN 23, 1936	WATER	WOOD
Rat (Water)	JAN 24, 1936	- FEB 10, 1937	WATER	FIRE
Ox (Earth)	FEB 11, 1937	- JAN 30, 1938	EARTH	FIRE
Tiger (Wood)	JAN 31, 1938	- FEB 18, 1939	WOOD	EARTH
Rabbit (Wood)	FEB 19, 1939	- FEB 7, 1940	WOOD	EARTH
Dragon (Earth)	FEB 8, 1940	- JAN 26, 1941	EARTH	METAL
Snake (Fire)	JAN 27, 1941	- FEB 14, 1942	FIRE	METAL
Horse (Fire)	FEB 15, 1942	- FEB 4, 1943	FIRE	WATER
Sheep (Earth)	FEB 5, 1943	- JAN 24, 1944	EARTH	WATER
Monkey (Metal)	JAN 25, 1944	- FEB 12, 1945	METAL	WOOD
Rooster (Metal)	FEB 13, 1945	- FEB 1, 1946	METAL	WOOD
Dog (Earth)	FEB 2, 1946	- JAN 21, 1947	EARTH	FIRE
Boar (Water)	JAN 22, 1947	- FEB 9, 1948	WATER	FIRE
Rat (Water)	FEB 10, 1948	- JAN 28, 1949	WATER	EARTH
Ox (Earth)	JAN 29, 1949	- FEB 16, 1950	EARTH	EARTH
Tiger (Wood)	FEB 17, 1950	- FEB 5, 1951	WOOD	METAL
Rabbit (Wood)	FEB 6, 1951	- JAN 26, 1952	WOOD	METAL
Dragon (Earth)	JAN 27, 1952	- FEB 13, 1953	EARTH	WATER
Snake (Fire)	FEB 14, 1953	- FEB 2, 1954	FIRE	WATER

ANIMAL	CHINESE NEW YEAR DATES	EARTHLY BRANCH	HEAVENLY STEM
Horse (Fire)	FEB 3, 1954 - JAN 23, 1955	FIRE	WOOD
Sheep (Earth)	JAN 24, 1955 - FEB 11, 1956	EARTH	WOOD
Monkey (Metal)	FEB 12, 1956 - JAN 30, 1957	METAL	FIRE
Rooster (Metal)	JAN 31, 1957 - FEB 17, 1958	METAL	FIRE
Dog (Earth)	FEB 18, 1958 - FEB 7, 1959	EARTH	EARTH
Boar (Water)	FEB 8, 1959 - JAN 27, 1960	WATER	EARTH
Rat (Water)	JAN 28, 1960 - FEB 14, 1961	WATER	METAL
Ox (Earth)	FEB 15, 1961 - FEB 4, 1962	EARTH	METAL
Tiger (Wood)	FEB 5, 1962 - JAN 24, 1963	WOOD	WATER
Rabbit (Wood)	JAN 25, 1963 - FEB 12, 1964	WOOD	WATER
Dragon (Earth)	FEB 13, 1964 - FEB 1, 1965	EARTH	WOOD
Snake (Fire)	FEB 2, 1965 - JAN 20, 1966	FIRE	WOOD
Horse (Fire)	JAN 21, 1966 - FEB 8, 1967	FIRE	FIRE
Sheep (Earth)	FEB 9, 1967 - JAN 29, 1968	EARTH	FIRE
Monkey (Metal)	JAN 30, 1968 - FEB 16, 1969	METAL	EARTH
Rooster (Metal)	FEB 17, 1969 - FEB 5, 1970	METAL	EARTH
Dog (Earth)	FEB 6, 1970 - JAN 26, 1971	EARTH	METAL
Boar (Water)	JAN 27, 1971 - FEB 14, 1972	WATER	METAL
Rat (Water)	FEB 15, 1972 - FEB 2, 1973	WATER	WATER
Ox (Earth)	FEB 3, 1973 - JAN 22, 1974	EARTH	WATER
Tiger (Wood)	JAN 23, 1974 - FEB 10, 1975	WOOD	WOOD
Rabbit (Wood)	FEB 11, 1975 - JAN 30, 1976	WOOD	WOOD
Dragon (Earth)	JAN 31, 1976 - FEB 17, 1977	EARTH	FIRE
Snake (Fire)	FEB 18, 1977 - FEB 6, 1978	FIRE	FIRE
Horse (Fire)	FEB 7, 1978 - JAN 27, 1979	FIRE	EARTH
Sheep (Earth)	JAN 28, 1979 - FEB 15, 1980	EARTH	EARTH
Monkey (Metal)	FEB 16, 1980 - FEB 4, 1981	METAL	METAL
Rooster (Metal)	FEB 5, 1981 - JAN 24, 1982	METAL	METAL
Dog (Earth)	JAN 25, 1982 - FEB 12, 1983	EARTH	WATER

ANIMAL	CHINESE NEW YEAR DATES		EARTHLY BRANCH	HEAVENLY STEM
Boar (Water)	FEB 13 1983	- FEB 1, 1984	WATER	WATER
Rat (Water)	FEB 2, 1984	- FEB 19, 1985	WATER	WOOD
Ox (Earth)	FEB 20, 1985	- FEB 8, 1986	EARTH	WOOD
Tiger (Wood)	FEB 9, 1986	- JAN 28, 1987	WOOD	FIRE
Rabbit (Wood)	JAN 29, 1987	- FEB 16, 1988	WOOD	FIRE
Dragon (Earth)	FEB 17, 1988	- FEB 5, 1989	EARTH	EARTH
Snake (Fire)	FEB 6, 1989	- JAN 26, 1990	FIRE	EARTH
Horse (Fire)	JAN 27, 1990	- FEB 14, 1991	FIRE	METAL
Sheep (Earth)	FEB 15, 1991	- FEB 3, 1992	EARTH	METAL
Monkey (Metal)	FEB 4, 1992	- JAN 22, 1993	METAL	WATER
Rooster (Metal)	JAN 23, 1993	- FEB 9, 1994	METAL	WATER
Dog (Earth)	FEB 10, 1994	- JAN 30, 1995	EARTH	WOOD
Boar (Water)	JAN 31, 1995	- FEB 18, 1996	WATER	WOOD
Rat (Water)	FEB 19, 1996	- FEB 6, 1997	WATER	FIRE
Ox (Earth)	FEB 7, 1997	- JAN 27, 1998	EARTH	FIRE
Tiger (Wood)	JAN 28, 1998	- FEB 15, 1999	WOOD	EARTH
Rabbit (Wood)	FEB 16, 1999	- FEB 4, 2000	WOOD	EARTH
Dragon (Earth)	FEB 5, 2000	- JAN 23, 2001	EARTH	METAL
Snake (Fire)	JAN 24, 2001	- FEB 11, 2002	FIRE	METAL
Horse (Fire)	FEB 12, 2002	- JAN 31, 2003	FIRE	WATER
Sheep (Earth)	FEB 1, 2003	- JAN 21, 2004	EARTH	WATER
Monkey (Metal)	JAN 22, 2004	- FEB 8, 2005	METAL	WOOD
Rooster (Metal)	FEB 9, 2005	- JAN 28, 2006	METAL	WOOD
Dog (Earth)	JAN 29, 2006	- FEB 17, 2007	EARTH	FIRE
Boar (Water)	FEB 18, 2007	- FEB 6, 2008	WATER	FIRE
Rat (Water)	FEB 7, 2008	- JAN 25, 2009	WATER	EARTH
Ox (Earth)	JAN 26, 2009	- FEB 13, 2010	EARTH	EARTH
Tiger (Wood)	FEB 14, 2010	- FEB 2, 2011	WOOD	METAL
Rabbit (Wood)	FEB 3, 2011	- JAN 22, 2012	WOOD	METAL

ANIMAL	CHINESE NEW YEAR DATES	EARTHLY BRANCH	HEAVENLY STEM
Dragon (Earth)	JAN 23, 2012 - FEB 9, 2013	EARTH	WATER
Snake (Fire)	FEB 10, 2013 - JAN 30, 2014	FIRE	WATER
Horse (Fire)	JAN 31, 2014 - FEB 18, 2015	FIRE	WOOD
Sheep (Earth)	FEB 19, 2015 - FEB 7, 2016	EARTH	WOOD
Monkey (Metal)	FEB 8, 2016 - JAN 27, 2017	METAL	FIRE
Rooster (Metal)	JAN 28, 2017 - FEB 15, 2018	METAL	FIRE
Dog (Earth)	FEB 16, 2018 - FEB 4, 2019	EARTH	EARTH
Boar (Water)	FEB 5, 2019 - JAN 24, 2020	WATER	EARTH
Rat (Water)	JAN 25, 2020 - FEB 11, 2021	WATER	METAL
Ox (Earth)	FEB 12, 2021 - JAN 31, 2022	EARTH	METAL
Tiger (Wood)	FEB 1, 2022 - JAN 21, 2023	WOOD	WATER
Rabbit (Wood)	JAN 22, 2023 - FEB 9, 2024	WOOD	WATER
Dragon (Earth)	FEB 10, 2024 - JAN 28, 2025	EARTH	WOOD
Snake (Fire)	JAN 29, 2025 - FEB 16, 2026	FIRE	WOOD
Horse (Fire)	FEB 17, 2026 - FEB 5, 2027	FIRE	FIRE
Sheep (Earth)	FEB 6, 2027 - JAN 25, 2028	EARTH	FIRE
Monkey (Metal)	JAN 26, 2028 - FEB 12, 2029	METAL	EARTH
Rooster (Metal)	FEB 13, 2029 - FEB 2, 2030	METAL	EARTH
Dog (Earth)	FEB 3, 2030 - JAN 22, 2031	EARTH	METAL
Boar (Water)	JAN 23, 2031 - FEB 10, 2032	WATER	METAL
Rat (Water)	FEB 11, 2032 - JAN 30, 2033	WATER	WATER
Ox (Earth)	JAN 31, 2033 - FEB 18, 2034	EARTH	WATER
Tiger (Wood)	FEB 19, 2034 - FEB 7, 2035	WOOD	WOOD
Rabbit (Wood)	FEB 8, 2035 - JAN 27, 2036	WOOD	WOOD
Dragon (Earth)	JAN 28, 2036 - FEB 14, 2037	EARTH	FIRE
Snake (Fire)	FEB 15, 2037 - FEB 3, 2038	FIRE	FIRE
Horse (Fire)	FEB 4, 2038 - JAN 23, 2039	FIRE	EARTH
Sheep (Earth)	JAN 24, 2039 - FEB 11, 2040	EARTH	EARTH
Monkey (Metal)	FEB 12, 2040 - JAN 31, 2041	METAL	METAL

ANIMAL	CHINESE NEW YEAR DATES	EARTHLY BRANCH	HEAVENLY STEM
Rooster (Metal)	FEB 1, 2041 - JAN 21, 2042	METAL	METAL
Dog (Earth)	JAN 22, 2042 - FEB 9, 2043	EARTH	WATER
Boar (Water)	FEB 10, 2043 - JAN 29, 2044	WATER	WATER
Rat (Water)	JAN 30, 2044 - FEB 16, 2045	WATER	WOOD
Ox (Earth)	FEB 17, 2045 - FEB 5, 2046	EARTH	WOOD
Tiger (Wood)	FEB 6, 2046 - JAN 25, 2047	WOOD	FIRE
Rabbit (Wood)	JAN 26, 2047 - FEB 13, 2048	WOOD	FIRE
Dragon (Earth)	FEB 14, 2048 - FEB 1, 2049	EARTH	EARTH
Snake (Fire)	FEB 2, 2049 - JAN 22, 2050	FIRE	EARTH
Horse (Fire)	JAN 23, 2050 - FEB 11, 2051	FIRE	METAL
Sheep (Earth)	FEB 12, 2051 - JAN 31, 2052	EARTH	METAL
Monkey (Metal)	FEB 1, 2052 - FEB 18, 2053	METAL	WATER
Rooster (Metal)	FEB 19, 2053 - FEB 7, 2054	METAL	WATER
Dog (Earth)	FEB 8, 2054 - JAN 27, 2055	EARTH	WOOD
Boar (Water)	JAN 28, 2055 - FEB 14, 2056	WATER	WOOD
Rat (Water)	FEB 15, 2056 - FEB 3, 2057	WATER	FIRE
Ox (Earth)	FEB 4, 2057 - JAN 23, 2058	EARTH	FIRE
Tiger (Wood)	JAN 24, 2058 - FEB 11, 2059	WOOD	EARTH
Rabbit (Wood)	FEB 12, 2059 - FEB 1, 2060	WOOD	EARTH
Dragon (Earth)	FEB 2, 2060 - JAN 20, 2061	EARTH	METAL
Snake (Fire)	JAN 21, 2061 - FEB 8, 2062	FIRE	METAL
Horse (Fire)	FEB 9, 2062 - JAN 28, 2063	FIRE	WATER
Sheep (Earth)	JAN 29, 2063 - FEB 16, 2064	EARTH	WATER
Monkey (Metal)	FEB 17, 2064 - FEB 4, 2065	METAL	WOOD
Rooster (Metal)	FEB 5, 2065 - JAN 25, 2066	METAL	WOOD
Dog (Earth)	JAN 26, 2066 - FEB 13, 2067	EARTH	FIRE
Boar (Water)	FEB 14, 2067 - FEB 2, 2068	WATER	FIRE

For All Your Feng Shui Needs Visit Our Flagship Boutique at World Of Feng Shui Mid Valley, KL, Malaysia

 **MALAYSIA**

WOFS MID VALLEY
3rd Floor, Centre Court, K.L.
Tel: +603-2287 9975
Email: wofs@worldoffengshui.com

WOFS NORTHPOINT
17th Floor, Northpoint Office,
Northpoint Mid Valley City, K.L.
Tel: +603-2080 3488
Email: wofs@worldoffengshui.com

WOFS ALOR SETAR
2nd Floor, Complex Star Parade,
Kedah. Tel: +604-730 8118
Email: alorsetar@worldoffengshui.com

WOFS BUKIT RAJA
Jusco Bukit Raja, Klang.
Tel: +603-3341 3889
Email: bukitraja@worldoffengshui.com

WOFS GURNEY
Plaza Gurney, Penang, Malaysia.
Tel: +604-228 4618
Email: gurney@worldoffengshui.com

WOFS IPOH
Jalan Theatre, Ipoh, Perak.
Tel: +605-249 2688
Email: ipoh@worldoffengshui.com

WOFS JOHOR
Ground Floor, Jusco Permas Jaya
Shopping Centre, Johore Bahru.
Tel: +607-388 9968
Email: johor@worldoffengshui.com

WOFS KOTA KINABALU
2nd Floor, Wisma Merdeka,
Kota Kinabalu, Sabah.
Tel: +088-248 798
Email: kotakinabalu@worldoffengshui.com

WOFS KUANTAN
1st Floor, Berjaya Megamall, Kuantan,
Pahang. Tel: +609-508 3168
Email: kuantan@worldoffengshui.com

WOFS KUCHING
Ground Floor, Wisma Ho Ho Lim,
Kuching, Sarawak, East M'sia.
Tel: +082-425 698
Email: kuching@worldoffengshui.com

WOFS MELAKA
Mahkota Parade, Melaka.
Tel: +606-282 2688
Email: melaka@worldoffengshui.com

WOFS MIRI
Level 1, Bintang Plaza, Miri.
Email: miri@worldoffengshui.com

WOFS MUTIARA
Ground Floor, Mutiara Hotel Johor
Bahru. Tel: +607-331 9968
Email: johor@worldoffengshui.com

WOFS PUCHONG
2nd Floor, IOI Mall, Puchong, Selangor.
Tel: +603-5882 2652
Email: puchong@worldoffengshui.com

WOFS SEREMBAN
1st Floor, Jusco Shopping Centre,
Seremban 2, Seremban. Tel: +606-601 3088
Email: seremban@worldoffengshui.com

WOFS SUBANG
Ground Floor, Subang Parade, P.J.
Selangor. Tel: +603-5632 1428
Email: subang@worldoffengshui.com

WOFS TAIPING
12A, Taiping Business Centre, Taiping,
Perak. Tel: +605-806 6648
Email: taiping@worldoffengshui.com

WOFS TEBRAU
2nd Floor, Aeon Tebrau Shopping
Centre, J.B. Johor. Tel: +607-357 9968
Email: johor@worldoffengshui.com

World of Feng Shui Head Office
A-17-1, 17th Floor, Northpoint Office, Northpoint Mid Valley City,
No.1, Medan Syed Putra Utara, 59200 Kuala Lumpur, Malaysia.
Tel: +603-2080 3488   Fax: +603-2287 4813
Email: letters@wofs.com

INTERNATIONAL

 ### AUSTRALIA
WOFS MELBOURNE
Lower Ground Floor, Crown
Entertainment Complex, Melbourne,
Victoria, Australia. Tel: +613-9645-8588
Email: melbourne@worldoffengshui.com

 ### BELGIUM
WOFS BELGIUM
Ninoofsesteenweg, Brussels, Belgium.
Tel: +32 02 522 2697
Email: belgium@worldoffengshui.com

 ### BRUNEI
WOFS BRUNEI
Warisan Mata-Mata, Brunei
Darussalam. Tel: +673-245 4977
Email: brunei@worldoffengshui.com

 ### CANADA
WOFS TORONTO
Rutherford Road, Tuscany Place at
Vaughan Mills, Vaughan, Ontario,
Canada. Tel: +1 905 660 8899
Email: toronto@worldoffengshui.com

 ### INDIA
WOFS CALCUTTA
Shakespeare Sarani, Calcutta, India.
Tel: +9133-22815263
Email: calcutta@worldoffengshui.com

 ### INDONESIA
WOFS ARTHA GADING
Artha Gading Mall, Gramedia Book
Store Jakarta-Utara.
Tel: +6221-668 3610/20/30
Email: indonesia@worldoffengshui.com

WOFS KELAPA GADING
Kelapa Gading Plaza, Jakarta
Indonesia. Tel: +6221-4526986
Email: indonesia@worldoffengshui.com

WOFS MATRAMAN
Toko Buku Gramedia Matraman,
Jakarta Timur, Indonesia.
Tel: +6221-8517325
Email: indonesia@worldoffengshui.com

WOFS MTA
Mall Taman Anggrek (MTA) Ground
Level Lt. Slipi-Jakarta Barat,
Indonesia. Tel: +6221-5699-9488
Email: indonesia@worldoffengshui.com

WOFS PLUIT
TB Gramedia Mega Mall Pluit, Jakarta
Utara. Tel: +6221-4586 4070
Email: indonesia@worldoffengshui.com

 ### JAPAN
WOFS JAPAN
S1 Nihonbashi Building SF 1-3-16
Nihonbashi Horidomecho Chuocity
Tokyo Japan. Tel: +81-3-5645-6680
Email: japan@worldoffengshui.com

WOFS MIE
670-2 Shinmei Ago-Cho Shima-City,
Mie,517-0502, Japan.
Tel:+81-599-43-8909
Email: mie@worldoffengshui.com

 ### NETHERLANDS
WOFS NETHERLANDS
Stationsplein 1, Netherlands.
Tel:+31-356781838
Email: netherlands@worldoffengshui.com

 ### PHILIPPINES
WOFS CEBU
Lower Ground Floor, SM City Cebu,
Philippines. Tel: +032 231 4088
Email: philippines@worldoffengshui.com

WOFS PHILIPPINES
Ground Floor, The Podium,
Mandaluyong City, Metro Manila,
Philippines. Tel: +63-29106000
Email: philippines@worldoffengshui.com

WOFS MOA
Mall of Asia, SM Central Business Park
1, Island A, Bay City, Pasag City.
Tel: +63-2910 6000
Email: philippines@worldoffengshui.com

WOFS SM NORTH EDSA
The Block, Quezon City, Philippines.
Tel: +63-856 0669
Email: philippines@worldoffengshui.com

WOFS SERENDRA
The Piazza, Fort Bonifacio,
Global City, Philippines.
Tel: +63-856 0669
Email: philippines@worldoffengshui.com

 ### RUSSIA
WOFS MOSCOW
Office 6-8, Building 519,
Russian Exhibition Center, Moscow,
129515, Russian Federation.
Email: moscow@worldoffengshui.com

 ### SPAIN
WOFS BARCELONA
C.Urgell, Barcelona, Spain.
Tel:+34934244801
Email: spain@worldoffengshui.com

WOFS MADRID
Centro Comercial Mercado Puerta
de Toledo, Madrid, Spain.
Tel: +34-91-3642771
Email: madrid@worldoffengshui.com

WOFS VALENCIA
Calle Joaquin Costa 53,
Valencia, Spain.
Email: valencia@worldoffengshui.com

 ### SINGAPORE
WOFS SINGAPORE
1 Harbourfront Walk, #B2 - 12,
Vivo City, Singapore 098585
(In front of Giant Hypermall)
Email: singapore@worldoffengshui.com

 ### THAILAND
WOFS SEACON SQUARE
2nd Floor, Seacon Square
Department Store, Thailand.
Tel: +66 (0) 2-721-9398
Email: bangkok@worldoffengshui.com

WOFS THAILAND
10th Floor, Regent House, Bangkok,
Thailand. Tel: +66 (0) 2-254-9918,
+66 (0) 2-254-7243, +66 (0) 2-254-9540
Email: bangkok@worldoffengshui.com

WOFS UNION MALL
F1 Union Mall Department Store 54,
Bangkok, Thailand.
Tel: +66(0)2-939-3268
Email: bangkok@worldoffengshui.com

 ### UNITED KINGDOM
WOFS LONDON
Whiteleys Shopping Centre,
Queensway.
Email: london@worldoffengshui.com

 ### UNITED STATES OF AMERICA
WOFS ARCADIA
Westfield Shopping Mall-Santa Anita,
Arcadia, CA, USA. Tel: +626 447 8886
Email: arcadia@worldoffengshui.com

WOFS HAWAII
Kilohana Square, Honolulu, USA.
Tel: +1808-739-8288
Email: hawaii@worldoffengshui.com

WOFS PEARLRIDGE
Uptown II, Monlua Road, Aiea,
Hawaii. Tel: +808-487-3888
Email: pearlridge@worldoffengshui.com

WOFS LAS VEGAS
Spring Mountain Blvd, Las Vegas, NV,
USA. Tel: +702-386-1888
Email: lasvegas@worldoffengshui.com

 ### VIETNAM
WOFS VIETNAM
Cong Hoa, Ward 4 District Tan Binh,
Ho Chi Minh, Vietnam.
Email: vietnam@worldoffengshui.com

For More Feng Shui Tips, News, Stories,
Activators & An Archive Of Feng Shui Articles,
Visit The World's Most Popular Website On Feng Shui
Consistently Ranked Number One
By Google & Microsoft at

www.wofs.com